S0-CRS-934

# REMARKS

ON THE

# STATISTICS AND POLITICAL INSTITUTIONS

OF THE

# UNITED STATES

# REMARKS

ON THE

# STATISTICS AND POLITICAL INSTITUTIONS

OF THE

# UNITED STATES,

WITH

SOME OBSERVATIONS ON THE ECCLESIASTICAL SYSTEM OF AMERICA, HER SOURCES OF REVENUE, &c.

TO WHICH ARE ADDED

STATISTICAL TABLES, &c.

BY

WILLIAM G. OUSELEY, ESQ.
ATTACHE TO HIS MAJESTY'S LEGATION AT WASHINGTON.

BOOKS FOR LIBRARIES PRESS
FREEPORT, NEW YORK

First Published 1832
Reprinted 1970

STANDARD BOOK NUMBER:
8369-5340-1

LIBRARY OF CONGRESS CATALOG CARD NUMBER:
70-117887

PRINTED IN THE UNITED STATES OF AMERICA

# INTRODUCTION.

Englishmen are accused by the Americans of viewing their country only through a medium of strong and generally hostile prejudice, or of describing it with intentional misrepresentation. Those who are obnoxious to such imputations are little likely to allow their justice; men do not readily confess their prejudices, and bad faith is still less easy of conviction. In either case, a *tu-quoque* of mutual recrimination is generally the only result of unmeasured censure. Of any intention to mislead the reader of the following remarks, on the subject of the United States, I need hardly say that I am utterly unconscious. The statements now published are, almost without exception, supported by the authorities of able writers. Whether I am liable to the accusation of prejudice must be decided by the judgment of others.

It is allowable, however, to state, that if my countrymen are justly chargeable with suffering their opinions to be biassed by the peculiar feelings and prepossessions of England, on leaving it for the first time, I am less likely than many others to have been influenced by such a circumstance. From early youth the far greater part of my life has been passed out of England, and in the diplomatic service of my country; and before my visit to America I had seen most of the countries of Europe.

Yet still it must be confessed that I did not arrive in the United States without having imbibed some of those preconceptions on the subject of the American political system that are so generally current in Europe. Judging from what had been witnessed in this hemisphere, it appeared to me that whatever might be said of the theory of the political system of America, yet in practice it could not succeed for any length of time, and that in Europe its imitation would be fraught with mischief and anarchy.

Those impressions of the practical inapplicability of the institutions of the United States to European nations have not been removed by a residence in that country; at least, the total unfitness of a republican government for adoption in England still appears to me incontrovertible. But the results produced *in America*, by her political system, are very different from those which one is led to expect by the representations of many, and some distinguished writers; and it has been my endeavour to point out a few of the reasons and facts which, in my mind, produced a conviction that the probabilities of success to the "great experiment" now in progress in the trans-atlantic republic were not to be measured by a scale formed from the circumstances of our own country.

It is not possible in the limits of a small volume like this, to give more than an outline of the various points touched upon in the following pages; many of the subjects mentioned are but incidentally and remotely connected with the nature of my profession; but the notice of them may serve to direct better qualified observers, in future publications on the affairs of America.

The communication with the United States is now so rapid and easy (the voyage often not occupying more than seventeen or eighteen days), that travellers may visit the principal cities of the Union and return to Europe within the space usually allotted for a summer excursion. The facility for frequent intercourse between the two countries must conduce to mutual advantages: it must, at all events, tend to dispel such prejudices on either side of the Atlantic as are the result of misconception or misrepresentation. Between countries the most dissimilar, and which for centuries have regarded one another as natural and national enemies, the facilities of communication have contributed to render the very term "natural enmity" an almost obsolete expression, applicable only to the ignorant and impolitic barbarism of past ages.

Whatever information may be afforded by this Essay, or by works of a far higher order, on subjects connected with America, they cannot tend to remove either wilful prejudice, or mistaken impressions, nearly so well as even a short visit to the United States:

> (" Segnius irritant animos demissa per aurem,
> Quam quæ sunt oculis subjecta fidelibus;")

where, whatever deficiencies may be perceived by

those accustomed to the life of an European capital, it must be allowed that a wide and interesting field is open to the research and observation of the statesman, the politician, the philosopher, or the practical man of business.

Although not immediately connected with the subject of this publication, I cannot forbear saying a few words on a topic deserving of the deepest consideration in this country, and of which the importance has only of late years been duly appreciated. The North American colonies furnish England with similar, and almost equivalent, advantages to those which the Americans possess in the superabundance of fertile territory, and consequent provision for its population generally, but particularly for the poorer and lower classes of society.

From my own observations in Canada and Nova Scotia, I have no hesitation in affirming, that to a moral certainty,—as well ascertained as any circumstance can be by human experience,—the moderately industrious and sober, however poor, are sure of obtaining not only a plentiful subsistence, but many comforts to which, in the present state of the commercial, manufacturing, and agricultural interests, they must in all probability long be strangers in the mother country. There is but one circumstance that might prevent the emigrant from realizing these fair prospects,—the loss of health. But in a climate so very salubrious as that of British North America, the probability of this evil is more remote than that to which, under circumstances of privation, he would be exposed in England. He will also find, I think, that the physical and positive advantages are more encouraging to the settler in Upper Canada, &c. than in the United States; independently of the reluctance that every right-minded Englishman must feel to abandon the colours of his country. He may be said to be nearly at home in the North American colonies.

"Cœlum non animum mutant, qui trans mare currunt."

By facilitating the means of emigration to the poorer classes of Englishmen, the British government would, perhaps, contribute as efficaciously to their welfare as by the extension of their political rights; and would probably find, in the vast resources of the North American colonies, a means of practically awarding "the greatest share of happiness to the greatest number" of our countrymen.

W. G. O.

*May* 7, 1832.

N.B. The works and authorities that have furnished data for these remarks, besides those quoted, are the Laws of the United States, American Almanac (Boston), Register of Department of State, Sword's Almanac and Ecclesiastical Register, Quarterly Register of American Education Society, Statistical Views by Watterston and Van Zandt, and American Congressional and State Papers, in addition to private notes, &c.

The tables in the Appendix do not pretend to perfect correctness: whoever may make an experiment in obtaining precise and accurate returns upon the subjects here treated, will find that it is neither an easy, nor very seductive task.

## CONTENTS.

### CHAPTER I.



### CHAPTER II.



### CHAPTER III.



### CHAPTER IV.

## CHAPTER V.



## CHAPTER VI.



## CHAPTER. VII.



## CHAPTER VIII.

## CHAPTER IX.



## CHAPTER X.



## CHAPTER XI.



## CHAPTER XII.



## CHAPTER XIII.

## CHAPTER XIV.



## CHAPTER XV.



## CHAPTER XVI.



## CHAPTER XVII.



## CHAPTER XVIII.

# APPENDIX.

# APPENDIX

# REMARKS

ON

# THE STATISTICS, &c.

OF

# THE UNITED STATES.

## CHAPTER I.

Introductory.—Misconceptions on the subject of America in Europe.—Contradictory accounts of travellers.—Arguments suited to European governments not often applicable to the United States.—Government of that country well adapted to the circumstances of its inhabitants.

Although the attention of Europeans, since the conclusion of the treaty of Ghent in 1814, has been directed to the progress of the United States of North America with more interest than at former periods, and although the rapidly increasing population and resources of the federal union have been of late years more justly appreciated than heretofore, yet there is perhaps no country of equal importance that is in fact so little known in Europe generally. No better proof can be wanting of this ignorance in our country, on the subject of America, than the conflicting and contradictory opinions and reports concerning it that are continually made public. Not only the allusions frequently made in either house of parliament to the theoretic tendency and practical effects of her political institutions, but the observations of the daily and periodical press furnish ample evidence of the great difference of opinion that exists on the advantages or defects of her form of government, and its influence on the social system in some measure its consequence.

That many misconceptions as to the real situation of the Americans should be entertained by those who have never visited their country is the less surprising, when we observe that, even among the numerous travellers in the United States who have published their impressions of its present condition, or their views of its future prospects, there should be such diversity of opinion, that one is sometimes inclined to doubt that the different writers are describing the self-same country. This may doubtless be said of accounts of other countries; but, where intercourse is frequent, and distance from our homes not great, vulgar errors are rectified, or prejudiced mistatements contradicted, with greater facility and certainty than where that serious obstacle to an intimate acquaintance between two nations intervenes, viz. some thousand miles of the Atlantic.

Even those rapid improvements in the means of communication anticipated by some* sanguine authors will not so speedily overcome this natural bar to an intimate acquaintance with the American continent, as not to allow for many years to come a wide field for speculation and theoretical discussion, founded on partial and exaggerated statements, and unintentional or wilful misrepresentation.

While one party, zealously admiring the system of America, represents the United States as a political Utopia, and would wish to transplant her institutions and particularly her financial economy to England, forgetful of the many circumstances rendering such a form of government or any such practical adoption of her scale of expenditure *undesirable or impossible in this country*,—another set of men are unceasing in their condemnation of every thing American, describing manifold evils as the present effects, and predicting convulsion and ruin as the future results, of the mode of government which the people of the United States have adopted. In either case the *ignotum pro magnifico* accounts for the

* Vide M'Gregor's British America, M'Taggart's work, &c.

exaggerated opinions so frequently, and often conscientiously, expressed on the subject.

But the opinions of travellers in the United States, however speculative, deserve more attention than those of men who write by their firesides strictures upon countries of which they have no practical knowledge, and whose impressions are coloured by the prejudices of a party, or their own misapprehensions. Unfortunately, those who have published descriptions of America have not generally remained there long enough to be enabled to use their judgment uninfluenced by prepossessions against or in favour of the theory or practice of the American system; they consequently apply a scale of their own, adapted to a country widely different in circumstances, manners, and institutions, in forming opinions of the government and people of the United States. The traveller who on first arriving in any foreign country should unreservedly commit to paper his impressions and opinions of its usages or political institutions, and endeavour to explain and account for its peculiar customs, from his own observations and knowledge, and then lay aside his notes during a year's residence in the same place, would probably be surprised on a reperusal of them at the mistaken views that he had in many instances taken; at least I have found it so. And if this be true of European countries, having generally many features of resemblance, it is particularly so in the judgments passed by Europeans on the United States. I am speaking now more especially of the political institutions of America, but the same remarks are even more strikingly applicable to the social system of that country. It should be recollected that many provisions of the constitution of the United States, which to an Englishman appear at first sight fraught with danger, will perhaps on a nearer examination be found well adapted to the *American Union;* for we are prone unconsciously to apply the arguments that would be good in England to a country extremely dissimilar; and thus contemplating, with views and ideas suited to a very different state of things, particular measures or modes of government, it is not surprising that our judgments and predictions of their consequences should be erroneous. Americans say that we look at their republican institutions through our "monarchical spectacles," and that it requires some apprenticeship to so different a state of things to see them in their true light.

Let us look at the converse of this proposition. When an American arrives in England for the first time, he is apt to jump at conclusions equally unfounded respecting our country. I know what were the impressions of some individuals from the

United States, and men of sagacity and experience, on first witnessing the practical workings of our constitutional monarchy, and the results of our social system. And if most Americans were honestly to confess their real opinions (formed after only a short residence in England) at any period during the last thirty years, I am convinced that there are few who would not avow a conviction of their astonishment at the possibility of our government having continued to work with any success for five years together; but after a residence of greater duration, they perceive the existence of counteracting causes preventing many of the bad effects which they anticipated, and even begin to think that the transition to a form of government like their own would neither be so easy nor so advantageous as they previously believed. Americans are eminently practical men; all their undertakings, and generally all the measures, whether of governments or individuals in that country, are stamped with utility as their object, and dicated by sound practical good sense and prudence. They consequently quickly detect the wildness and absurdity of many of the republican theories of those Europeans, who would seek to adopt forms of government totally unfitted for the circumstances of their country;—and soon adapt their views to the peculiarities of the political atmosphere in which they find themselves.

Englishmen do not, I think, so readily divest themselves of their preconceived ideas when reflecting on the situation of America, and are apt to continue bigoted in their own hypotheses, notwithstanding the frequent contradictions from facts and practical results to which they are continually subjected. It would be difficult otherwise to account for the erroneous views that are so often taken of the American republic; and for the condemnation of a system pursued with such remarkable success in one country, because it is not adapted to the circumstances of another.

As all human institutions carry with them from the first moment of their origin the seeds of their own decay or dissolution, it would be folly to expect that the American constitution should not share in the general imperfection of our nature. But so far from considering the political system of the United States as *peculiarly* fraught with danger to its own existence, and built upon imprudently slight foundations, I conceive it to be better adapted for the security, good government, and welfare of the American people, than any which could perhaps, under their peculiar circumstances, have been conceived; indeed this opinion is supported by the authority of writers by no means friendly to popular governments.* The constitution of America was the work of the combined talent and experience of men of sagacity and information, well acquainted with the wants and habits of their own country, and not ill versed in the theories or practices of others; and they constructed their institutions upon a foundation of experience and practical ability, to suit the peculiar circumstances of their countrymen. Hitherto their system has worked wonderfully for the prosperity of the United States, and it is not one of its least advantages that any necessary change or amelioration is foreseen and provided for with such careful precautions and restrictions, as prospectively secure a remedy for future wants or changes of circumstance. It appears, I think, likely to last, and adapt itself to the mutations brought on by the lapse of years, with at least as fair a prospect of success as the nature of most human institutions can promise.

* Vide Quarterly Review, No. XCII. p. 585. "It is a scheme, indeed, with which the Americans may well be content; for one *better fitted to their situation* it might not have been very easy, if possible, to devise."

## CHAPTER II.

Nature of American republic generally misunderstood in Europe. —Its dissimilarity to the republics of antiquity, or to those of more modern times.—Contrasts between the American republic and that which succeeded the first French revolution.—Of a federal union.

The name of *republic*, or rather the associations connected with that title, may go a great way in accounting for the misconceptions and prejudices with which all considerations of the government of the United States are observed. Most of our recollections of school and college connected with the word *republic*, present the classical images, but really rude and uncivilized habits, of Sparta, the vices and defects of Athens or Lacedemonia, or the fluctuating and turbulent æras of Rome. Whatever may have been the boyish enthusiasm in favour of those governments of antiquity, inspired by the nature of our early course of education, there are few of us who have assumed the toga of manhood without discovering that no forms of government could be well imagined less adapted to the wants, the habits, or the religious lights of our own country in the present day, than the political systems of Greece or

Rome; and that they would be as little suited to work well in modern times, as the forms of their mythological divinities would be to decorate an altar in our temples. We soon perceive that the continual internal warfare and divisions of the rival petty states of Greece were as unlikely to conduce to the happiness of mankind as the continual struggles between the patrician and plebeian parties in Rome.

The name of republic, as applied to the governments of Italy, contributed still farther to the condemnation of that form of government. The patricians and princely merchants of the north of Italy might wear the mask of republicans for the support of their anomalous or commercial oligarchies —with almost equal justice might the East India Company's government at Calcutta be called a republic, at least as that term is understood in America; and the former government of Holland is scarcely less dissimilar.

But general opinion as to the nature of the government of the United States has been more influenced by the misnomer of republic having been assumed by the sanguinary and tyrannical leaders of the French revolution of the last century, than by any of the foregoing attempts at popular governments in the annals of history. When the word republic is mentioned, straightway a train of horrors is called up in the minds of most Europeans. Murder, rapine, violence and anarchy, and all the accompaniments of the reign of terror, with atheism and sacrilege at their head, are conjured into existence, and crowd the picture which we draw of the effects and nature of a republican government.

Locke advises us to take care accurately to define *words*, by which means we shall avoid much disputing about *things*. If the word republic be applicable to any of the governments alluded to above, and particularly to the monstrous and impracticable attempt of the French Jacobins, *then* is the government of the United States not *a republic*, but requires some other designation.

Instead of sanguinary executions and injustice, we find in America a penal code singularly mild, and cautious to an extreme in taking away human existence; a system of punishment framed with a view to the prevention of crime, and not in a vindictive spirit; and adapted for the reclamation of the criminal rather than for his destruction.* Instead of spolia-

* The excellent of the penitentiary system of the United States has been frequently noticed by late travellers in America. The penal laws are sometimes blamed by the advocates of a Draconic code as being too mild. The following extract from a report of the Society for the Improvement of Prison Discipline is better than a comment upon the results of the different systems:—" The amount of crime in proportion to population is as follows:—In England, 1 criminal in 740; Wales, 1 in 2320; Ireland, 1 in 490;

tion or pillage, we see no country in which the possession and disposal of property are better protected, or its acquisition by judicious industry better assured. And above all, there is no country in which religion and its ministers are more generally respected and supported by the mass of the population, although without compulsory provision, and where the lives and example of the clergy more nearly approach to those of their great primitive models.*

In examining the nature of the transatlantic republic, we find not the astute tyranny of an Italian aristocracy, nor the abuses of usurped power; neither do we witness the conflicts between an insatiate populace and a proud and unfeeling nobility, as in Rome; while the internal struggles, the want of

Scotland, 1 in 1130; Denmark, 1 in 1700; Sweden, 1 in 1500; in New South Wales, 1 in 22; while in the United States it is 1 in 3500."

* "We had abundant ocular demonstration of the respect paid to the subject of religion;"—"scarcely a village, however small, without a church," &c.—Vide *Capt. B. Hall's Travels in United States*, Vol. I. p. 151, and elsewhere.

With regard to the accounts lately published by a female traveller in America, if we *were even to allow that* they are faithful descriptions, and not satirical caricatures, it would be about as fair to estimate the church system of England by the proceedings of a meeting of Jumpers or Ranters in some remote village, or by the hallucinations of the followers of Johanna Southcote, as to judge of the ministers and followers of different denominations in America by the representations of Mrs Trollope.

Some account of the revenues, &c. of the clergy of the United States will be found in a subsequent chapter.

unity and force, are obviated by a federal* union, unknown to the republics of antiquity.

We may perhaps expect, arguing from what we see of the violence of contested elections at home, that they must, *a fortiori*, be attended with tumult and riot a thousandfold worse in a country where something nearly approaching to universal suffrage exists,

* Paley thus speaks of a federal republic :—" We have been accustomed to an opinion, that a republican form of government suits only with the affairs of a small estate." After then enumerating several of the objections usually urged against republican governments, he proceeds :—

" Add to these considerations, that in a democratic constitution the mechanism is too complicated, and the motions too slow, for the operations of a great empire, whose defence and government require execution and despatch, in proportion to the magnitude, extent and variety of its concerns. There is weight, no doubt, in these reasons, *but much of the objection seems to be done away by the contrivance of a federal republic*, which distributing the country into districts of a commodious extent, and leaving to each district its internal legislation, reserves to a convention of the states, the adjustment of their relative claims; the levying, direction and government of the common force of the confederacy; the requisition of subsidies for the support of this force; the making of peace and war; the entering into treaties; the regulation of foreign commerce; the equalization of duties upon imports, so as to prevent the defrauding of the revenue of one province by smuggling articles of taxation from the borders of another; and likewise so as to guard against undue partialities in the encouragement of trade. To what limits such a republic might, without inconveniency, enlarge its dominions by assuming neighbouring provinces into the confederation; or how far it is capable of uniting the liberty of a small commonwealth with the safety of a powerful empire; or whether, amongst co-ordinate powers, dissensions and jealousies would not be likely to arise, which, for want of a common superior, might proceed to fatal extremities;

whereas we find that, compared with our assemblies, the elections of the United States are order itself, pelting, mobbing, or brawling, are almost unheard of on such occasions, and more than all, there is little or no bribery, or possibility of succeeding *merely by dint of money.*

are questions upon which the records of mankind do not authorize us to decide with tolerable certainty. The experiment is about to be tried in America upon a large scale."—Vide Paley, "*Of Different Forms of Government,*" chap. vi.

## CHAPTER III.

Supposed defects of American form of goverment examined.—Proneness to war.—National feelings towards England.—M. de Talleyrand's observations on that subject.—M. Politica.—Advice of Washington on the foreign policy to be adopted by the United States.

Many objections have been made to the political system of the United States, founded generally upon certain theories, or deduced from observations on the results of governments called republics that have already existed. The principal defects attributed to the form of government adopted in America are these:—that the preponderance of the democratic party in the state will force the government into wars and aggressions upon other countries, particularly where national antipathies or predilections exist—that the representatives chosen by the mass of the people become mere delegates, whose abilities and judgments are fettered by the popular will—that property must be insecure under such circumstances, and that none but men of low origin and unfitted for high situations will be elected by the classes forming the numerical majority of votes in the United States—that the judicial powers in the state will lose their independence—and that the alleged economy of the American government is a delusion which only requires some examination of facts to dispel.

First, as to the warlike propensities attributed to republican governments, it is evident that the institutions of the United States are not obnoxious to an accusation founded upon a supposed resemblance between the United States and the French republic of the last century. Capt. B. Hall makes some judicious remarks upon this subject when speaking of the possibility of a future invasion of the Canadas.* A country that, with a population of 13,000,000, finds a standing army of 6000 men† sufficiently large for all its purposes, is unlikely to embark in wars of ambition, if even territorial acquisition were thought requisite for its strength, which is certainly not the case with America. For the purposes of defensive warfare, there is perhaps no country more formidably provided than the United States at the present day. In 1827, their militia,

* See also Paley. "The advantages of a republic are, liberty, or exemption from needless restrictions; equal laws; regulations adapted to the wants and circumstances of the people; public spirit; frugality; *averseness to war*, *&c.*" Paley on *Different Forms of Government.*

† It is somewhat singular that the number of pensioners (all military, as there are no civil pensions granted in the United States) should greatly exceed that of the whole army. They still amount to 16,324, principally men who were engaged in the revolutionary war.

almost precisely similar to the national guard of France in its organization, amounted to upwards of 1,150,000, and all parties agree that few countries are better prepared to resist foreign invasion.*

On the other hand, aggressive wars are little likely to be undertaken by a country so opposed to heavy taxation as America, and where such powerful obstacles exist to the dangerous or unconstitutional ambition of any military leader. It has been asserted that any popular demonstration of national jealousy, or dislike of a particular country, would hurry a republican administration into warlike measures upon slight grounds, and that in the United States such hostility would be more likely to display itself against Great Britain than any other power, from the alleged dislike and antipathy pervading all classes towards England and Englishmen. The evidence of this feeling, as regards individuals, cannot be found in many works of late writers, however hostile to the political institutions of America; on the contrary, it is only necessary to open almost any chapter of Capt. Hall's Travels, of Mr de Roos's or M. Vigne's, &c.,†

* The Quarterly Review admits this, *more suo:* "The nation may be compared to a great sand-bank, of which all the particles may be good enough in themselves, but which, *except for the purpose of destroying any one who attempts to meddle with them*, have no principle of joint action," &c.—Vide Quarterly Review, No. XCIII. March, on "Domestic Manners of the Americans."

† Capt. Basil Hall, Vol. III. p. 2. "The same kindness and

to find a testimony in favour of the hospitality, the ready and obliging assistance, perfect good-will and civility generally shown to English travellers, which from my own personal experience, and that of my friends, I can fully corroborate. It is indeed so strong as to have been observed at a period when political and national feelings were roused, and not

hospitality were shown to us here (at Washington) as elsewhere;" &c. &c. Further on, "we never discovered the slightest diminution of that attention by which we had already been so much flattered during the journey;" and many other passages might be cited from this gentleman's travels to prove the good feeling prevalent towards Englishmen in the United States.

Mr Stanley, soon after his return from the United States, used the following language in the house of commons:—"So strong were the ties of a common origin, that an English gentleman travelling in that great republic is sure to meet with the most hospitable reception, as he well knew by personal experience, that great country was proud to acknowledge its relationship to England, and to recognize the love and attachment it yet felt to the mother country, and would feel for ages."

Capt. de Roos thus expresses his opinion on this subject:—"Nothing can be *more unfounded* than the notion which is generally entertained, that a feeling of rancour and animosity against England and Englishmen pervades the United States."

"Though vilified in our journals, and ridiculed upon our stage, they will be found upon a nearer inspection to be brave, intelligent, kind-hearted, *and unprejudiced;* though impressed with an ardent, perhaps an exaggerated, admiration of their own country, they speak of others without envy, malignity, or detraction." And again:—'One introduction is sufficient to secure to an Englishman a general and cordial welcome."—"At New York the character of an Englishman is a passport," &c.—"At a public *table d'hote*, we were treated with the greatest civility by the promiscuous party, *who drank the king's health* out of compliment to our nation," &c. &c.—Vide also M'Gregor, &c.

unjustly,* and the passions enlisted against Englishmen by the unfortunate effects of warfare with other powers.

* "To place the full annoyance of these matters in a light to be viewed by English people, let us suppose that the Americans and French were to go to war, and that England for once remained neutral—an odd case, I admit, but one which might happen. Next, suppose that a couple of French frigates were chased into Liverpool, and that an American squadron stationed itself off that harbour to watch the motions of these French ships, which had claimed the protection of our neutrality, and were accordingly received into 'our waters,' I ask, 'would this blockade of Liverpool be agreeable to us, or not?'

"Even if the blockading American frigates did nothing but sail backwards and forwards across the harbour's mouth, or occasionally run up and anchor abreast of the town, it would not, 'I guess,' be very pleasant to be thus superintended. If, however, the American ships, in addition to this legitimate surveillance of their enemy, were to detain off the port, with equal legitimacy of usage, and within a league or so of the light-house, every British ship coming from France, or from a French colony, and if, besides looking over the papers of these ships, to see whether all was regular, they were to open every private letter, in the hope of detecting some trace of French ownership in the cargo, what should we say? And if, out of some twenty ships arrested daily in this manner, one or two ships were to be completely diverted from their course, from time to time, and sent off under a prize-master to New York for adjudication, I wonder how the Liverpool folks would like it? But if, in addition to this perfectly regular and usual exercise of a belligerent right on the part of the Americans, under such circumstances we bring in that most awkward and ticklish of questions, the impressment of seamen, let us consider how much the feelings of annoyance, on the part of the English neutral, would be augmented.

"Conceive, for instance, that the American squadron employed to blockade the French ships in Liverpool was short-handed, but from being in daily expectation of bringing their enemy to action,

One of the most powerful causes of the favourable feeling towards Englishmen is of course to be found in the common origin of the two people. But an-

it had become an object of great consequence with them to get their ships manned; and suppose, likewise, that it were perfectly notorious to all parties, that on board every English ship arriving or sailing from the port in question there were several American citizens, but calling themselves English, and having in their possession protections or certificates to that effect, sworn to in a regular form, but well known to be false, and such as might be bought for 4*s*. 6*d*. any day. Things being in this situation, if the American men-of-war off the English port were then to fire at and stop every ship, and, besides overhauling her papers and cargo, were to take out any seaman to work their own guns withal whom they had reason, or supposed, or said they had reason to consider American citizens, or whose country they guessed from dialect or appearance;—I wish to know with what degree of patience this would be submitted to on the exchange at Liverpool, or elsewhere in England?

"It signifies nothing to say that such a case could not occur, as the Americans do not impress seamen; for all who have attended to such subjects know well enough that if they come to be engaged in a protracted war, especially at a distance from their own shores, there is no other possible way by which they can keep their armed ships manned. This, however, is not the point now in discussion. I merely wish to put the general case broadly before our own eyes, in order that we may bring it distinctly home to ourselves, and then see whether or not the Americans had reason for their indignation."—*Vide Capt. Basil Hall's Fragments of Voyages and Travels, p.* 174, *first series.*

It would, perhaps, not be easy to induce an American to concede the possible necessity of impressment; but that is not the question at present. Captain Hall places the whole subject of the irritations which contributed so materially to hasten the last war between Great Britain and the United States before the public so fully and impartially in this very interesting little work, that I cannot refrain from continuing my extracts. He proceeds to say (page 299):

other great moral influence and bond of union is a community of language. In a "Memoir" written by the present French ambassador at this court, which deserves to be as well known in England as it is in America, are the following very remarkable observations:—

"In putting a parallel case to ours off New York, and supposing Liverpool to be blockaded by the Americans on the ground of their watching some French ships, I omitted to throw in one item which is necessary to complete the parallel, and make it fit the one from which it is drawn.

"Suppose the blockading American ships of Liverpool, in firing a shot a-head of a vessel they wished to examine, had accidentally hit, not that vessel, but a small coaster so far beyond her, that she was not even noticed by the blockading ships; and suppose further this unlucky chance shot to have killed one of the crew on board the said coaster, the vessel would of course proceed immediately to Liverpool with the body of their slaughtered countryman; and, in fairness it may be asked, what would have been the effect of such a spectacle on the population of England, more particularly if such an event had occurred at the moment of a general election, when party politics, raging on this very question of foreign interference, was at its height?

"This is not an imaginary case, for it actually occurred in 1804, when we were blockading the French frigates in New York. A casual shot from the Leander hit an unfortunate sloop's main-boom; and the broken spar striking the mate, John Pierce by name, killed him instantly. The sloop sailed on to New York, where the mangled body, raised on a platform, was paraded through the streets, in order to augment the vehement indignation, already at a high pitch, against the English.

"Now, let us be candid to our rivals, and ask ourselves whether the Americans would have been worthy of our friendship, or even of our hostility, had they tamely submitted to indignities which, if passed upon ourselves, would have roused not only Liverpool, but the whole country, into a towering passion of nationality?"

"Identity of language is a fundamental relation on whose influence one cannot too deeply meditate. This identity places between the men of England and America *a common character which will make them always take to, and recognise each other*. But an insurmountable barrier is raised between people of a different language, who cannot utter a word without recollecting that they do not belong to the same country; betwixt whom every transmission of thought is an irksome labour, and not an enjoyment; who never come to understand each other thoroughly, and with whom the result of conversation, after the fatigue of unavailing efforts, is to find themselves mutually ridiculous."*

After detailing some of the effects of the great moral influence of the use of the English language on the legislative and political institutions of the United States, M. de Talleyrand says, that "we must renounce all knowledge of the influence of laws upon man, and deny the modifications which he receives from all that surrounds him, if we do not concede the immense influence which the use of a common language has upon inter-national relations."

The personal observations of this acute statesman are further confirmed by M. Politica, formerly the

* American translation.

representative of Russia in North America, in his "*Aperçu*" on the United States, in which he bears witness to the great moral effects on the social institutions, habits, and feelings of America, to be ascribed to the unavoidable use of the language of the mother country.

It may be said that this feeling can exist towards individuals without influencing the councils of a nation. But whatever may have been the feelings of animosity that, at an earlier period of the existence of the American union as an independent government, pervaded its members, any person can form an opinion, from the publicity with which the affairs of the United States are transacted, whether traces of such hostile feelings are more to be perceived in the measures of the present government of that country, than in the behaviour of individuals, or the acts of our own government. It would have been better, perhaps, for all countries if the advice of that great and excellent man, General Washington, had been considered as applicable to other forms of government as to that United States.

In the address of the first president of the United States to his fellow-citizens, on declining to be considered a candidate for their future suffrages, are these excellent recommendations:

"Observe *good faith* and *justice* towards all nations; *cultivate peace and harmony* with all. Religion and morality enjoin this conduct; and can it be that good policy does not equally enjoin it? It will be worthy of a free, enlightened, and (at no distant period) a great nation to give to mankind the magnanimous and novel example of a people always guided by an exalted justice and benevolence. Who can doubt that, in the course of time and things, the fruits of such a plan would richly repay any temporary advantages which might be lost by a steady adherence to it? Can it be that providence has not connected the permanent felicity of a nation with virtue? The experiment, at least, is recommended by every sentiment which ennobles human nature. Alas! is it rendered impossible by its vices?

"In the execution of such a plan, nothing is more essential than that *permanent, inveterate antipathies against particular nations, and passionate attachment for others, should be excluded;* and that, in the place of them, just and amicable feelings towards all should be cultivated. The nation which indulges towards another an *habitual hatred*, or an *habitual fondness*, is in some degree a slave. It is a slave to its animosity, or to its affection; either of which is sufficient to lead it astray from its duty and its interest. *Antipathy in one nation against another, disposes each more readily to offer insult and injury,* to lay hold of *slight causes of umbrage*, and to be haughty and intractable when accident or trifling occasions of dispute occur. Hence frequent collisions, obstinate, envenomed and bloody contests. The *nation*, prompted by ill-will and resentment, sometimes *impels to war the government*, contrary to the best calculations of policy. The government sometimes participates in the national propensity, *and adopts, through passion, what reason would reject;* at other times, it makes the animosity of the nation subservient to projects of hostility, instigated by pride, ambition, and other sinister and pernicious motives. The peace often, sometimes perhaps the liberty, of nations has been the victim.

"So, likewise, a passionate attachment of one nation for another produces a variety of evils. Sympathy for the favourite nation, facilitating the illusion of an imaginary common interest, in cases where no real common interest exists, and infusing into one the enmities of the other, betrays the former into a participation in the quarrels and wars of the latter, without adequate inducement or justification. It leads also to concessions to the favourite nation of privileges denied to others, which is apt doubly to injure the nation making the concessions, by unnecessarily parting with what ought to have been retained; and by exciting jealousy, ill-will, and a disposition to retaliate in the parties from whom equal privileges are withheld: and it gives to ambitious, corrupted, or deluded citizens (who devote themselves to the favourite nation) facility to betray or sacrifice the interests of their own country without odium, sometimes even with popularity; gilding with the appearances of a virtuous sense of obligation, a commendable deference for public opinion, or a laudable zeal for public good, the base or foolish compliances of ambition, corruption, or infatuation."

He further says:—

"The great rule of conduct for us in regard to foreign nations is, in extending our commercial relations, to have with them as little *political* connexion as possible. So far as we have already formed engagements, let *them be fulfilled* with *perfect good faith.* Here let us stop.

"Europe has a set of primary interests, which to us have none, or a very remote relation. Hence she must be engaged in frequent controversies, the causes of which are essentially foreign to our concerns. Hence, therefore, it must be unwise in us to implicate ourselves by artificial ties in the ordinary vicissitudes of her politics, or the ordinary combinations and collisions of her friendships or enmities.

"Our detached and distant situation invites and enables us to pursue a different course. If we remain one people, under an efficient government, the period is not far off when we may defy material injury from external annoyance; when we may take such an attitude as will cause the neutrality we may at any time resolve upon to be scrupulously respected; when belligerent nations, under the impossibility of making acquisitions upon us, will not lightly hazard the giving us provocation; when we may choose peace or war, as our interest, guided by justice, shall counsel.

"Why forego the advantages of so peculiar a situation? Why quit our own to stand upon foreign ground? Why, by interweaving our destiny with that of any part of Europe, entangle our peace and prosperity in the toils of European ambition, rivalship, interest, humour, or caprice?

"It is our true policy to steer clear of permanent alliances with any portion of the foreign world; so far, I mean, as we are now at liberty to do it; for let me not be understood as capable of patronising infidelity to existing engagements. I hold the maxim no less applicable to public than to private affairs, that honesty is always the best policy. I repeat it, therefore, let those engagements be observed in their genuine sense. But, in my opinion, it is unnecessary, and would be unwise, to extend them.

"Taking care always to keep ourselves by suitable establishments in a respectable defensive posture, we may safely trust to temporary alliances for extraordinary emergencies.

"Harmony, and a liberal intercourse with all nations, are recommended by policy, humanity, and interest. But even our commercial policy should hold an equal and impartial hand; neither seeking nor granting exclusive favours or preferences," &c. &c. &c.

Without here examining whether the different administrations of America have always acted strictly in accordance with these wise suggestions, we at least see in them an explanation of the motives that induce the United States sedulously to avoid "entangling alliances," which in *their peculiar position* it would be folly to contract. And in the adoption of the line of policy here recommended to America, it is to be hoped will be found an antidote to such national enmities as may be supposed to exist in the councils of that country.

## CHAPTER IV.

Examination of objections to the political institutions of the United States continued.—Effects of very large constituencies not such as have been anticipated.—Corruption not general.—The representative bodies in America not *de facto* delegates.

WITH respect to the assumption, that large constituencies, formed upon the principles that are in force in America, will return unworthy representatives, it is not found to be confirmed by the experience of several years, even in the larger states, and where the greatest extension is given to the democratic principle. We are also apt to suppose in England, that where multitudes of voters have to decide the elections, a necessary consequence will be extreme disorder, riot, and confusion; I can only say, that from whatever cause, no such effects generally arise from the mode of elections in the United States. Let us take New York for an example. And here I shall quote the statements of a correspondent of one of the leading journals of this country, which, as far as my opportunities of observation allow me to judge, are perfectly correct on this head. The letter is written in support of the clause, giving additional representatives to the metropolis; and after anticipating the objections, on the score of riot, expense, &c., proceeds to state—

"But what in reality is the case? In a late warmly contested election to the senate for the state of New York, there were about 250,000 voters polled; there were no brickbats, no dead cats, or any similar arguments resorted to on either side; in short, such modes of election are unknown among our unpolished brethen, and the expense to the successful candidate was about 40*l.*

"But then 'the man who was elected was surely some greasy mechanic,—some pot-companion and worthy prototype of the illiterate and ignorant men who elected him?'

"The successful candidate was a man who has from early youth distinguished himself by his talents, his eloquence, and his enlarged and benevolent views. He occupied the post of secretary of state for the foreign and home departments, and relinquished that office from a high and delicate feeling of the peculiar position of his party, and that of the present president of the United States, to accept the appointment of minister to this country; in a word, it was Mr Van Buren.

"Nor is this a solitary instance, nor confined to one party; Mr Clay, Mr Webster, Mr M'Lane (the late envoy to this country), and indeed with scarcely an exception, all the men elected by the larger bodies of constituents, are men distinguished for their talents, their services, or their standing in the estimation of the country. Nor are we authorised to say, that this is peculiar to the inhabitants of the United States: human nature is much the same, whether on this side of the Atlantic or the other. Neither are men in the lower walks of life prone to elect as their representatives those in nowise their superiors. The thought, 'I am as good as he is,' will prevent it. On the contrary, the greater the multitude, the more elevated must be the position which it is necessary to take, in order to be advantageously in their view.

"Then, on the score of expense, the opponents of popular representation will say, 'you must advocate vote by ballot, or the influence of wealth will be paramount in this country, whatever it may be there.' But let them recollect, that it is not easy to buy the majority of 250,000 votes, at even 5*l.* each. And what is rather a remarkable fact, the ballot is, in a thousand instances, not resorted to in the United States; on the contrary, a display of the sentiments of the voters is made as much as in this country; and the order that prevails is less surprising, when we recollect who are the individuals here, whose arguments in support of their favourite candidate consist in the missiles thrown at the head of his opponent. Are they not very generally those who have no vote? A man feels that he can much more effectually support his representative by giving him his vote than by stopping the mouth of the other party with a cabbage or a dead cat; and he perfers the easier and more useful method."*

M. Vigne confirms this account of the difficulty of perpetrating any acts of corruption in the United States, and his conviction of the non-existence of bribery at elections generally, he says, "that although, supposing the rich sometimes to influence the poor voters, he believes votes are rarely bought in the United States:"—this is quite true, "voters are too numerous, and therefore corruptions costly and difficult of concealment;" and elsewhere, "it is to the credit of America that individual wealth *has never yet been employed* for any unconstitutional purpose."† I cannot join in giving this credit entirely to the self-denial or patriotic principle of the people of the United States. I look upon it as rather the result of their institutions, human nature being much the same, and subject to the same temptations, in America as elsewhere; but their whole political system has been devised with a view to depriving

* Times, March 3d, 1832.

† Vide Vigne's *Six Months in America*, Vol. I. p. 152 and 191; Vol. II. p. 242.

wealth of all but its *legitimate* advantages: and admirably have its framers succeeded. A *millionaire*, in America, may have a mansion in every capital of the union, establishments in town or country, on any scale he pleases of expense or luxury, and were he distinguished for talents or merit, his riches would, of course, *cæteris paribus*, give him certain advantages; but he would in vain attempt to procure admittance to either house of legislature, by *dint of wealth alone;* and I do not think that it would be possible to adduce a single instance to disprove this assertion.

It has been remarked that an aristocracy is growing up in every city in the union; but it should be remembered that it is not a *political*, but a *social* aristocracy.

The representatives in congress have been repeatedly described as mere delegates, and not free to exercise their opinions or abilities according to the dictates of their own judgment or conscientious intentions. But this, although, perhaps, considered theoretically true of the house of representatives, by a great proportion of the Americans, is disallowed by many others; and with regard to the senate, certainly does not hold good as a rule. It may be said that, *de facto*, the state of the question is very much the same as in England. On any great national question arising, or about to be decided, the electors naturally ascertain the sentiments of a candidate upon that particular subject, leaving him free to exercise his unpledged opinion upon all other topics that are not supposed so vitally to concern their immediate interests.

To say that every member of congress is, therefore, a mere delegate upon any debate that might arise would be an error, and, indeed, would in most cases be mistaking cause for effect. The representative is elected *because his opinion on certain subjects is known and approved*, not in order that he may be compelled to register prejudged decisions opposed to his own judgment.

I have before me at this moment a speech of Mr Clay's, upon a highly important subject, and find the following words:—"I stand here as the humble but zealous advocate, *not of the interests of one state, or several states only, but of the whole union;* and never before have I felt more intensely the overpowering weight of that share of responsibility which belongs to me in these deliberations," &c.: surely this is not the principle of a hard-curbed and hoodwinked delegate.*

In conversation with more than one of the most

* Vide Debates in the Senate, Feb. 1832.

distinguished men in congress, I have frequently heard opinions expressed that quite corroborated the view here taken of the state of feeling on this head in the United States.

Other objections on the score of insecurity to property, real expense of the government of the United States, &c. are incidentally answered in the course of the following pages; but with regard to the real independence of the judicial power of America, so vital a question deserves particular attention.

## CHAPTER V.

Supreme Court of the United States.—Its judicial independence and high character.—Diplomatic agents particularly interested in its proceedings.—Has jurisdiction in all cases touching the law of nations.—State "Judiciaries."—Associate judges.

It would be quite superfluous on the part of the author of these pages to offer any remarks upon the high personal and judicial character of the chief justice and the other individuals composing the supreme *court of the United States; such a tribute of respect, as he would be proud to offer, could only be regarded as a matter of course, by those who have been honoured by an acquaintance with these gentlemen; or who have regarded with any attention the proceedings of the court at which they preside.

But the elevated reputation which the decisions and conduct of the supreme court of the United States have so justly acquired, is by no means likely

* The character of the venerable Chief Justice Marshall is as justly appreciated and respected by those foreigners whose high diplomatic situations have afforded them opportunities of cultivating his friendship, as by his own countrymen. And it is a singular compliment extorted from those who are inimical to the institutions of his country, that they attribute much of the success that has hitherto attended its existence to the personal character of the head of the supreme court.

to cease with the lives of those now composing it. If judicial independence can be secured by any safeguard to be provided by legislative foresight or prudence, it will not be difficult to show that the federal "judiciary" of the United States is placed upon as firm a basis as can be well imagined.

The nature of the supreme court* of the United

* "That the supreme court shall have exclusive jurisdiction of all controversies of a civil nature, where a state is a party, except between a state and its citizens; and except also between a state and *citizens of other states, or aliens*, in which latter case it shall have original, but not exclusive jurisdiction; and shall have, exclusively, all such jurisdiction of suits or proceedings against *ambassadors, or other public ministers, or their domestics, or domestic servants*, as a court of law can have or exercise *consistently with the law of nations;* and original, but not exclusive jurisdiction of all suits brought by *ambassadors or other public ministers, or in which a consul or vice-consul shall be a party.*"—Public and General Statutes of the United States, published by Justice Story, chap. xx. § 13.

There are few countries where the immunities and privileges extended by civilized nations to the representatives of foreign powers, are more complete or more strictly protected than in America: thus, "if any writ or process shall, at any time hereafter, be sued forth or prosecuted by any person or persons, in any of the courts of the United States, or *in any of the courts of a particular state*, or by any judge or justice therein, respectively, whereby *the person of any ambassador or other public minister, of any foreign prince or state, authorized and received as such by the president of the United States, or any domestic or domestic servant of any such ambassador or other public minister, may be arrested or imprisoned, or his or their goods or chattels be distrained, seized, or attached*, such writ or process shall be deemed or adjudged to be *utterly null and void*, to all intents, construction, and purposes whatsoever.

States is the more interesting to foreigners, as it has original jurisdiction in all suits brought by foreign ministers, chargés-d'affaires, &c. It takes cognizance exclusively of all cases affecting envoys and other diplomatic functionaries, consuls, vice-consuls,

§ 26. "That in case any person or persons shall sue forth or prosecute any such writ or process, such person or persons, and all attorneys or solicitors prosecuting or soliciting in such case, and all officers executing any such writ or process, being thereof convicted, shall be deemed violators of the laws of nations, and disturbers of the public repose, *and imprisoned, not exceeding three years, and fined at the discretion of the court,*" *&c.* This protection is legally assured by a very easy condition, viz., that "the name of such servant be first registered in the office of the secretary of state, and by such secretary transmitted to the marshal of the district in which congress shall reside, who shall, upon receipt thereof, affix the same in some public place in his office, whereto all persons may resort and take copies without fee or reward."

§ 27. "That if any person shall violate any safe conduct or passport duly obtained, and issued under the authority of the United States, or shall assault, strike, wound, imprison, or in any other manner infract the law of nations, by offering violence to the person of an ambassador or other public minister, such person so offending, on conviction, *shall be imprisoned not exceeding three years, and fined at the discretion of the court.*"—Ibid., chap. xxxvi. § 25, 26 and 27. And the most extended and liberal interpretation is given to these provisions.

In a case that occurred soon after the assumption of the throne by Don Miguel in Portugal, a suit was instituted against one of the agents of Don Pedro, or rather Donna Maria. As this gentleman was no longer *legally* a representative (after the recognition of Don Miguel by the United States), it became a question of some interest and doubt, whether the usual privileges would be allowed in his case; but the utmost extension of national courtesy was exercised on this occasion, and all proceedings accordingly stopped.

as well as of all cases connected with the law of nations.

Some important peculiarities are observable in the relations of the United States with other governments, which result partly from the form of its constitution, and partly from legal causes. In the ratification of treaties, for instance, the concurrence of *two-thirds of the senators present* is required to carry into effect the ratification of the president of the United States.*

Difficulties also arise in procuring the delivery to the agents of a foreign power of fugitives from justice, &c., somewhat similar to those which the *habeas corpus* act produces in cases of a like nature in England. This was long ago perceived by a very intelligent observer of American affairs:—"Quoiqu'il en soit, une chose très-positive et qu'il importe de ne pas perdre de vue, lorsqu'on a des rapports politiques avec le gouvernement Américain, c'est que *sa souveraincté est incomplete.* Il en resulte que dans plusieurs cas, où le droit des gens est intéressé, il est impossible au gouvernement Américain d'accorder la reciprocité sans outre passer ses pouvoirs."†

* Vide Constitution of the United States, Art. II. sect. 2.

† However this may be, one thing is very certain, and must by no means be lost sight of in any political relations with the Ameri-

The members of the federal judiciary are appointed for life, and they can be dismissed from office only by impeachment. In England no judge can be removed but by conviction for some offence, or the *address of both houses of parliament*, which may be *called an act of legislature.* But the judges of the supreme court cannot be reached by address, and enjoy perfect immunity from the measures of either the president or the houses of congress. In some of the states, however, a similar provision to that of our constitution has been adopted, but the dangers to the practical independence of the judges, arising from popular excitement, have been neutralized by requiring the concurrence of *two-thirds* of each branch of the legislature, in order to effect a removal.

In some of the estates the judges are periodically elective: this I think must be considered as a vicious system, and many persons of experience will be found in the United States who much condemn it, and who regret that the organization is not universally assimilated to that of the judiciary of the federal government.

can government. *Its sovereign power is incomplete.* From which it results, that in many cases, where the law of nations is concerned, it is impossible for the American government to admit reciprocity, without exceeding its legal powers.—Politica's *Aperçu de la Situation interieure des Etats Unis d'Amerique*, p. 79.

There is one peculiarity of the state "judiciary" deserving of remark. Two *associate judges* are appointed, who assist a legal judge presiding on the bench of the courts of the various judicial districts: this has appeared to many foreigners as an injudicious anomaly in legal practice. I am not sufficiently cognizant of the subject to attempt to decide upon its technical propriety; but, practically, the results of this system are good. The associates being generally men of respectability and good sense, well acquainted with the local peculiarities of their districts, and engaged in the ordinary transactions of life, they may often modify the mere legal and strictly literal application of the laws. The presiding lawyer-judge, abstracted by professional pursuits from a similar familiarity with the common business and occupations of his fellow-citizens, has thus an opportunity of obtaining information on particular cases from two persons who may be regarded in some measure as *responsible jurors;* they may also be considered as answering many of the purposes of our magistrates, of whom by far the greater proportion are not legal men, and often very imperfectly qualified to decide on legal points; they are liable to greater responsibility however than our magistracy, and although sometimes acting *de facto* as equitable arbitrators, leave points of law to the professional judge. An appeal also lies from their decisions to the supreme court.

Captain Hall does not think that the independence of judicial functions in the United States is sufficiently assured. His remarks on the subject are so ably answered by the author of a "Review of Captain B. Hall's Travels in North America,"* that I must refer the reader to an extract from it, to be found in the Appendix,† for a much better elucidation of the subject than it is in my power to give.

It is to be regretted that Captain Hall should have so decidedly announced a determination never himself to adopt the old principle of *audi alteram partem* (on the subject of America), which he justly recommends to others; he might possibly have found that in some instances he has, from the unavoidable disadvantages under which all foreigners labour when describing in detail so extensive a country as the United States, misconceived some points in a moral and political system so very different from our own.

* Attributed, I believe rightly, to the president of the Bank of the United States, Mr Biddle,* a gentleman distinguished alike for sound sense, extensive information, and the pleasing urbanity of his manners.

† Vide Appendix, No. 1.

---

* *Note to American edition.* The author is R. Biddle, Esq.

Mr Vigne, whose opinions on this subject deserve greater weight from his being himself a lawyer, as well as from the generally unprejudiced tone of his pleasing work, says, "the authorities of the supreme court are intended as the safeguards of the union;" and he adds, justly, "that the independence of this court, and, in fact, of all the federal judiciary, may be termed the sheet anchor of the United States."

The late decision of the court in favour of the Cherokee Indians, and reversing a decree lately obtained by the state of Georgia, cannot but add to the dignified and impartial character that has ever distinguished the proceedings of that eminent body, and gives additional confidence, if any were wanting, in the future firmness of a court, whose principles are as unbiassed by selfish as by party feelings.

## CHAPTER VI.

Misrepresentations of the domestic manners of the Americans.—Many of the peculiarities of the social system of the United States not attributable exclusively to the republican form of government.—Advantages and defects compared of American and English systems.

It was not my intention to have touched upon the social system of the United States, or the effects produced upon it by the nature of its government; it is but incidentally connected with the object of these remarks. A late work, however, upon the "Domestic Manners of the Americans," has presented such a very unfaithful picture of society in the United States, that a few observations on the subject may be necessary. It is true that the authoress describes but the manners and habits of a portion of the community, and of a section of the country but lately emerged from the state of an almost uninhabited wilderness; while her candid declaration of dislike and ill-will towards the Americans and their institutions, political or social, sufficiently accounts for the satirical, clever, but highly coloured caricatures in which the writer indulges. But the general reader, amused by the spirited tone of acerbity and sarcastic talent with which the pictures are drawn, and totally unacquainted with the country described, does not examine the justice of the representation, as applied to the upper classes, particularly in the larger and older capitals, and mistakes it for a general outline of American society. This impression is fostered by the notice in the Quarterly Review, which carefully keeps out of view Mrs Trollope's raptures at New York, and even at Washington, in which places, however, it does not appear that she, from whatever cause, ever was received in the higher circles. Of Boston and New England, generally, which others* describe as, *par excellence*, the seat of ultra aristocracy in the United States, the work does not speak at all.

To estimate justly the fidelity of the writer's satire as a *tableau général* of American society in the United States, let us imagine an American, or any other foreigner, coming to England, and "locating" himself in the fens of Lincolnshire, or in some remote village of Lancashire† or Yorkshire, and giving the language, tone, and manners of the

* Vide Vigne, Vol. II. p. 242.

† Mr M'Gregor says, speaking of the United States, "no gentleman who is commonly polite will meet with any thing but kind treatment in America; and *as to the peculiarities of their tongue, I need only observe that I have never met with an American, however humble, whose language was not perfectly plain and intelligible to*

society that he might find there as a fair specimen of good company in England; or lodging at Wapping, or in some obscure part of the Tower Hamlets, and giving the "vells" and "vats," the "osses" and "himages" of some of the cockney population as a fair sample of London manners! He might even add, "I give this as a specimen of the manners and habits of the *greater part* of the community," with literal truth, as doubtless, numerically, the major part of the inhabitants of the metropolis do not distinguish themselves as *puristes* in language; but would it be strictly fair to convey such an impression of the general manners of England, if a faithful picture were intended? The late publication of the tour of prince Pückler Muskeau is a fulsome eloge of English usages compared with Mrs Trollope's account of American manners; yet it has not escaped censure neither the most gentle nor argumentative.

If the foreign traveller whom I am supposing, in addition to his bad choice of residence, should evince the equally bad taste of visiting England under the auspices of Mr Carlile or the "Rev." Mr Taylor, and come to pass some time under their roof, it would not contribute to render his subsequent ac-

*me; while I can scarcely understand half what the country people say within a few miles of me in Lancashire,"* &c.—Vide M'Gregor, Vol. I. p. 39.

cess to the best society more ready. It was doubtless unfavourable to the opportunities which the authoress herself could of course have easily commanded, of personally judging of the high classes of society in America, that some of her "philosophical friend's" "fanatical"* and "startling theories" were highly unpopular in the United States, and an intimacy with that lady was, possibly, not the best avenue to the society of the "patrician few" whose manners are *not* described by the authoress.

In Miss Wright's lectures, according to the Quarterly Review† and the newspaper reports upon them, she advocated the suppression of all religions, and the abolition of all such restraints upon the natural impulses, as the institution of marriage, &c. &c.

A strong prejudice exists in America, notwithstanding the supposed want of respect for all established customs, in favour of these antiquated institutions, and against the doctrines promulgated by Miss Wright; and, in a country where such a feeling is predominant, and where the women of the upper classes are accused of being prudishly sensitive

* The Quarterly, in reviewing Mrs Trollope's book, thus designates Miss Wright's attempts to preach down religion, marriage, &c.; while the poor German Prince is called a "blasphemer," a "scoffer," &c.—Vide Quarterly Review, Nos. XCII., XCIII., 1832.

† "Miss F. Wright, lecturer itinerant against Christianity, matrimony, and all other old-fashioned delusions," &c.—Ibid.

on all subjects where female delicacy is concerned, it is not difficult to conceive that her patronage was no passport to the best society. Mrs Trollope very properly condemns the system of Miss Wright, and in much stronger terms than the reviewer; but it is to be presumed that justice was not done to her on this score, or we should doubtless have seen in her book descriptions proportionately as graphic and faithful to the good society of America as her diatribes against the lower orders are severe and *chargées.* Judging by the high praise that she bestows on some portion* of what she saw in the United States, it is fair to suppose that she would have done justice to a very different state of society from that which she describes, had she enjoyed opportunities of personally forming an opinion on the habits of the upper ranks.

As to the more classical refinements produced by the cultivation of a taste for the fine arts, and the elaborate luxuries which naturally arise in a community where hereditary wealth and rank give leisure and encouragement to the lighter and more seductive studies, they cannot be expected to attain rapidly to any perfection, when the very culture of the soil is in its infancy. But it is surprising that where

* Vide her Descriptions of New York, Washington, beauty of the women, &c. &c.

pursuits and occupations, little connected with literary and scientific pursuits, are of necessity so universally followed, there should, in the older Atlantic capitals at least, be such progress already made towards these ornamental superstructures of civilization. *Le superflu, chose si necessaire*, may be found either at Boston, New York, Philadelphia, &c., and in much greater perfection that might reasonably be expected by Europeans; those who are disappointed at not finding the "stately homes of England" rising among primeval forests, or on the banks of rivers that but a few years back watered the undisturbed domain of the painted Indian, have in truth built castles in the air when they proceeded to visit America. And if we find little artificial and conventional refinement among persons enjoying many of those comforts of affluence that among us are generally the portion of the few and educated alone, should we not rather consider the complete independence and comparative happiness of a large class of men, who in the mother country might be starving on the miserable stipend of a poor-house, or on the daily wages of fifteen hours' work in a manufactory, than be surprised at their rusticity of manner? It is quite true, that many of the habitual elegances of life (which a very few years ago were exotic superfluities in our own country) are not tò be met with in the recently settled countries, and there are "men of education and of refinement,* in every state of the union," who know by the experience acquired in other countries, the full value of the advantages that they cannot expect as yet to realize in their own. But let us pause awhile, and reflect, that if we listen to the predictions of those who argue the speedy downfall of the political institutions of America, we should also await the lapse of a few years of successful improvements, to pronounce on the possibility of refinement following in the steps of wealth and education, especially in that country, where a comparatively very short period suffices to produce a wonderful advancement. Nor should we attribute all the defects incident to the infancy of every society entirely to the effects of the popular nature of the government of the United States. The inhabitants of the contemporaneous colonies of British America,† under similar physical circumstances, evince the same aversion for menial service, from like causes, and have not been more distinguished in the career of literature, arts and sciences, than their immediate neighbours, although under a very different form of government; nor can it for some time be expected that it should be otherwise.

* Vide Vigne, Vol. II. p. 242.

† Vide B. Hall's Travels in North America, Vol. I. p. 229, &c.

If there are not, however, in America, generally, whether colonial or independent, many of the advantages which hereditary rank and privileged wealth *indisputably bring in their train*, neither are there their countervailing evils; political corruption, for instance, is nearly impracticable; if the conventional forms and increasing artificial wants of the highly artificial system of England are wanting, neither is there to be discovered that much more disgusting and contemptible real vulgarity resulting from the abject worship of rank and wealth that debases the lower orders, and some members of almost every class of society in our country. If the roughness of manner and extreme independence of the lower classes* in the remote

* There are many parts of Europe where the freedom of manner of the lower classes would much startle a cockney traveller, particularly in nations where Englishmen are inclined to think that a great degree of personal degradation must necessarily be found among the *bourgeois* and peasantry. In Spain, Austria, Denmark, or Sweden, a traveller is frequently struck by this independence of deportment. I have witnessed it in all these countries, but particularly in Spain. In the mountains of Andalusia, in a hovel of a *venta*, the host, or his brother peasants, will receive you with perfect good-nature and rough hospitality, but with a cool tacit assertion of perfect equality in demeanour, as widely different from the habits of England as are those of America. It is true, that while eating garlic with a pocket-knife and with a lack of the means and appliances of civilized life that would be the death of a dandy, the lowest Spaniard has a quiet dignity of manner that, however rustic, must exclude vulgarity, which never can exist where there is a true and natural independence of

parts of the union be occasionally disagreeable to Europeans, accustomed to, and perhaps exacting, the interested homage paid to opulence in other countries, the *bassesses* with which exclusive divinities are propitiated in England (and verily often by those who have little excuse for not knowing better) are unknown. There may be much want of external polish found combined with much practical good sense; although there are few of the miserable coxcombries of dandyism,—there will be

feeling and absence of affectation. This freedom, or perhaps coarseness, of manner is not offensive (at least I never found it so), because you perceive in it an evident absence of all intentional incivility; yet it was, perhaps, more near being disagreeable sometimes in the *cafés* and larger *fondas* or inns, where the waiters when unemployed would quietly take their seats, after, perhaps, asking you to light their cigar with your own. I remember particularly on board one of the steam-boats that run between Cadiz and Seville (for steam-boats now are constructed on the banks of the Guadalquivir, and somewhat disenchant the reveries of the traveller), the waiter, with his cap on his head and stump of a cigarillo in his mouth, quietly seated himself by me and took one of my pistols from holsters lying near, and began coolly to descant on the merits of its English workmanship. I have been on board many American steam-boats, and never saw the theory of equality and independence so strongly exemplified by the practices of any of their attendants. There is a want of keeping in this sort of familiarity when in a crowded city or on board one of these floating hotels, at least our associations make us think so, that is infinitely more likely to give a slight feeling of what the French call *chair de poule*, than when we meet the active peasant on the mountain-paths of the Contrabandistas, or the athletic, well-armed, and well-mounted "caballero," who *may* be no better (*or no worse*) than a peasant, in the wild fastnesses of a Moorish village on the sierras of Andalusia.

found successful individuals of humble origin (not forming exceptions to a rule, but) in numbers sufficient to prove amply that talent and well-directed industry and energy are certain, as human institutions can make them, of being rewarded by the highest stations in society: yet it will not be easy to find among the numerous and efficient *employés* of the American government a single specimen of the genus, vulgarly, but expressively, classified as the "Jack-in-office," whose absurd or stupid impertinence often clogs the operations of the European bureaux that they infest. There are to be found men of large hereditary or acquired possessions, whose feelings, education and manners would ornament any society, divested of the puerile varieties of an exclusive circle, or the putid puppyisms of the silver-fork school.

Americans may well be excused if their patience is somewhat taxed by the short-sighted and captious criticisms that are sometimes uttered by foreigners upon their country, their government, or their manners. I look at that immense tract of country west of the Alleghanies, that a very few years ago was comparatively a wild forest, where many millions of acres were thinly occupied by a *few thousand inhabitants, and see a population already greater than that of several independent kingdoms, daily increasing in numbers and adding to their comforts; where cities and towns spring up as if by magic from among the woods; its plains traversed by rail-roads and its gigantic rivers covered with steam-boats. I see all this going on without tumult, bloodshed, or disorder; and when I exclaim, "this is a noble, an extraordinary country!" I am answered in Abigail phrase—"but, shocking, the people eat with their knives!"

* "Witness the result of free and protecting institutions. Fifty years ago the population westward of the Alleghanies did not exceed 15,000, now it amounts to five millions. The population of priest-ridden Mexico has not increased for centuries."—*See Vigne, Vol. II. p. 85.*

## CHAPTER VII.

Financial and general prosperity of United States.—Its peculiar causes considered.—Principally attributable to a free and protecting government.—Mexican and South American republics compared with the United States.—Report of Mr M'Lane on the finances of the United States. Opinions of Revue Britannique and Quarterly Review on economy of American government.

THAT part of the American system which, perhaps, most strikes the European observer, is its excellent financial administration, and the success that has hitherto constantly attended all the fiscal arrangements of the union, as well as the continued increase of its sources of revenue not accompanied by a proportionate augmentation of expenditure. Again, if we turn from the contemplation of the revenue and expenses of the federal government to consider the general revenues of the United States as a nation, the growing prosperity and riches of each state, of companies, or individuals, we find generally an equally flourishing state of things.

Many peculiar but sufficiently obvious circumstances contribute to this unexplained prosperity. The virgin soil of immense and fruitful tracts of unoccupied territory awaiting the increasing wants of an enterprising and industrious population; the non-existence of powerful and jealous neighbouring governments; or, at least, of such as seek to interfere with the growing fortunes of the republic, or who have any interest in so doing; all the facilities for commercial undertakings that are afforded by the command of numerous excellent harbours, maritime cities, immense rivers, every material for ship-building, and the possibility of producing the growth of almost every soil or climate within their own territory:—these advantages, improved by the peculiar feelings, disposition, and habits, which I may be excused as an Englishman for thinking are inherited from the mother country,—all these contribute, together with many others that might be enumerated, to the unexampled progress of the extraordinary country that we are considering.

But although, when tracing the sources of this prosperity of the Transatlantic republic, due weight must be allowed for the co-operation of all the above causes in producing such successful results, we must not forget that they are mainly attributable to the free institutions adopted from the commencement of the existence of the United States as an independent government. This popular form of government may be said to have owed its origin and frame work to the system already in force when America formed part of the colonial possessions of Great Britain.

Nor can it be denied that the character of the people and their previous political *education* (if this term may be allowed), impressed with the habits, and familiar with the mechanism, of representative and free forms of government (one of their best inheritances from their British progenitors), had the greatest influence in forming the system that at present regulates the American federation, and produced the most beneficial effects in carrying into practice the principles adopted at its foundation.

The spirit that animates the institutions of the United States affords encouragement to all classes to improve each of the numerous resources within their reach; by facilitating* education and the diffusion of practical knowledge, the people are prepared to reap those advantages, the possession of which is afterwards protected by the force and stability of the laws. The results so far exceed the rational anticipations of even impartial observers, that in seeking to account for them, we are apt to undervalue the immense effects of free and protecting institutions in producing such gigantic consequences,

* Vide Appendix, List of Colleges, &c.

and thus ascribe an undue share in their production to the influence of other causes. Doubtless the adoption of the form of government of the United States would not have *alone* caused an increase of population from three to thirteen millions in fifty years, nor the absence of a national debt —nor would it have created such a maritime force and commercial navy as now exist in America; but, on the other hand, all the favourable circumstances to which we have alluded would not, under an opposite system, have produced similar prosperity.

Look at Mexico, for instance, favoured by climate (except on parts of the sea-coast or in the Gulf) beyond almost any country in the same latitude; and its productions of the richest and most profitable nature, with an immense and fertile territory: yet we see little promise, since the acknowledgement of her independence, of such a proportionate aggrandizement as the example of the United States might lead us to expect. Some of its richest and most available territory is at this moment occupied and brought into cultivation by a sort of private colony* of natives of the United States; and this with the connivance, if not protection and consent of the Mexican government, who rightly feel that

* For some account of this colony, and the province of Texas, see Appendix.

the resources of this important province (the Texas) will not soon be rendered available by their own people. If we look to the governments of South America, the results hitherto are still less encouraging, for the prospects of sudden emancipation (even under highly favourable physical circumstances) of a people not duly prepared to enjoy political independence.

It is true that some essential features of resemblance are wanting to render the parallel between the United States and South America complete. It has been objected that the South American republics form several distinct and independent countries, jealous of each other, and often as opposed by interests as different in habits; while, at the same time, they are separated by immense distances and natural obstacles. Yet the South American governments are more entirely the scions of the common stock than the states of the North American union,—they are almost exclusively of Spanish origin, speaking the same language and having the same religion; nor are they more disunited by distance, climate, or local interests, than the northern population of the United States are distinct from their southern fellow-citizens; added to which, many of the states of the union do not, even at the present day, assimilate either in language, habits, or religion.*

Why should the governments of South America not have worked so well as that of North America, unless from this want of previous habits of independence in the majority of the population, and a total ignorance of practical self-government? The same want of political experience was observ-

* New York was the Dutch colony of New Amsterdam, and at this moment many of the old Dutch families of New York are among the first in the union. On the occasion of a late visit of the minister of the King of Holland, M. Bangemann Huygens, to Albany, speeches and toasts, at dinners given to him in that capital, were made and replied to in the original language of the colony, which is still as familiar to many of the old families in New York as English; or, if we may rely upon the veracious History of Knickerbocker, much more so. In Pennsylvania, as well as many other states, there are great numbers of Germans, Swedes, and Finns, &c. or their descendants. In Louisiana, the language is principally French or Spanish; indeed many of the natives of that state do not understand English: in Florida, Spanish is general. The religion of the latter states is chiefly catholic: Maryland is also principally inhabited by catholics. In parts of New England the descendants of the puritans still retain much of their former strictness in religious duties. The followers of Penn are still numerous in Pennsylvania, and the tables in the Appendix will serve to show that there are about half as many different religious denominations as are enumerated by Evans in his "Sketch of the Denominations of the Christian World;" yet, notwithstanding these apparently discordant elements, the system of a federal union, combined with popular institutions, for which the majority of the population were previously prepared by their political education, has hitherto produced very different results from those of a similar experiment in South America.

able in many of the theorists of the liberal party who appeared in Spain at the time of the Cortez, and was one of the principal* *domestic* causes of its little internal stability.

A succinct and able *exposé* of the present state of the finances of the United States is to be found in the "Report" of Mr M'Lane (late envoy at this court, and now secretary of the treasury at Washington), submitted to congress last December. There are few nations who, at any period of their history, can refer to such an encouraging statement as is there given, or can look forward to fairer prospects of financial prosperity than are clearly presented by this report.

In this paper Mr M'Lane recommends the sale of certain stocks, held by the government of the United States, to the amount of eight millions of dollars; he having clearly shown that they possess the disposable means at present of reimbursing the whole of the public debt before the 3d of March 1833. The objects connected with the early reimbursement of the public debt being, as he justly remarks, more important than the interests of the government as mere stockholders.

* There is little doubt, however, that the foundation of a solid constitutional government would have been laid in Spain, but for the last interference of a foreign power to aid the views of one party in the state.

The obstacles to this arrangement consist in the inexpediency of throwing so large an amount into the public market, to obviate which a satisfactory arrangement with the Bank of the United States itself is suggested: and should his plans be adopted, the total annihilation of the public debt, on or before the 3d March 1833 may be effected; after which period, the amount of revenue applicable to that object will, of course, no longer be required. He thus comments upon this prospect:

"The moral influence which such an example would necessarily produce throughout the world, in removing apprehension, and inspiring new confidence in our free institutions, cannot be questioned. seventeen years ago our country emerged from an expensive war, incumbered with a debt of more than one hundred and twenty-seven millions, and in a comparatively defenceless state. In this short period it has promptly repealed all the direct and internal taxes which were imposed during the war, relying mainly upon revenue derived from imposts, and sales of the public domain. From these sources, besides providing for the general expenditure, the frontier has been extensively fortified, the naval and maritime resources strengthened, and part of the debt of gratitude to the survivors of the revolutionary war discharged. We have, moreover, contributed a large share to the general improvement, added to the extent of the union, by the purchase of the valuable territory of Florida, and finally, acquired the means of extinguishing the heavy debt incurred in sustaining the late war, and all remains of the debt of the revolution.

"The anxious hope with which the people have looked forward to this period, not less than the present state of the public mind, and the real interests of the community at large, recommend the prompt application of these means to that great object, if it can be done consistently with a proper regard for other important considerations."

Mr M'Lane proceeds to state that the estimated revenue for the expenditure of the government of the United States as at present authorized, need not exceed annually the very moderate sum of thirteen and a half millions of dollars. But he judiciously recommends appropriations in addition to this sum, for certain objects, some of which have long since excited the attention of all observers of American affairs, on either shore of the Atlantic, as urgently claiming the assisting care of the government of the United States. He thus enumerates the most prominent of these objects:

"For augmenting the naval and military resources; extending the armouries; arming the militia of the several states; increasing the pay and emoluments of the navy officers to an equality with those of the army, and providing them with the means of nautical instruction; enlarging the navy hospital fund; strengthening the frontier defences; removing obstructions from the western waters, for making accurate and complete surveys of the coast, and for improving the coasts and harbours of the union, so as to afford greater facilities to the commerce and navigation of the United States. The occasion would also be a favourable one for constructing custom-houses and warehouses in the principal commercial cities, in some of which they are indispensably necessary for the purposes of the revenue; and likewise providing for the proper, permanent accommodation of the courts of the United States and their officers.

"In many districts the compensation of the officers of the customs, in the present state of commerce, is insufficient for their support, and inadequate to their services. As a part of the general system, and effectually to guard the revenue, the services of such officers are necessary, without regard to the amount of business, and it is believed expedient to make their allowance commensurate with the vigilance required and the duties to be performed. A further improvement may be made in the mode of compensating the officers of the customs, by substituting salaries for fees in all the collection districts, by which, at a comparatively small expense to the treasury, commerce and navigation would be relieved from burthens, always inconvenient, if not oppressive.

"It is believed that the public property and offices at the seat of government require improvement and extension, and that further appropriations might be made to adapt them to the increasing business of the country.

"The salaries of the public ministers abroad must be acknowledged to be utterly inadequate, either for the dignity of the office, or the necessary comforts of their families. At some foreign courts,* and

* The salary of a minister from the United States to any foreign court is about 2000*l.*, with an outfit of the same sum. The consequence of this utter inadequacy of appointments, for supporting the position necessarily occupied by a foreign minister, either in London, Paris, Petersburgh, or Madrid, or any of the expensive residences is, that no minister will be found to remain long at any of these courts, unless he can afford to spend at least as much again as the salary from his government. In London, for instance, in the case of two American ministers, whose expenses I happened to know, it was obvious that half their appointments went to defray the expense of two items alone of their establishment, viz. house-rent and equipage. In Madrid there are many articles of comparatively trifling expense in other countries, that are there extremely expensive. The utter insufficiency of the salaries of the American foreign ministers has long been felt in the United States; but it is very difficult to make the members of congress from the remoter parts of the union com-

those whose relations towards the United States are the most important, the expenses incident to the station are found so burthensome, as only to be met by the private resources of the minister. The tendency of this is to throw those high trusts altogether into the hands of the rich, which is certainly not according to the genius of our system. Such a provision for public ministers as would obviate those evils, and enable the minister to perform the common duties of hospitality to his countrymen, and promote social intercourse between the citizens of both nations, would not only elevate the character of his country, but essentially improve its public relations.

"In addition to these objects, further provision

prehend the extreme difference in the scale of expenditure, absolutely necessary in Europe (to enable a foreign minister properly to support his position), from that to which they have been accustomed.

Mr M'Gregor, in his very useful work on British America, furnishes an additional proof, if any were wanting, of the extreme inaccuracy with which foreigners sometimes, with the best intentions, represent the affairs of other countries. Mr M'Gregor has every wish to do justice to the United States, and is generally very correct in his descriptions; we find, however, the following errors (possibly typographical). "The salary of the President is 25,000 *dollars*, or about 4,000*l*." (it is equivalent to between 5 and 6,000*l*.); Vice-President 5,000 *dollars*, or about 1,000*l*." (!) Afterwards he says, "Foreign ministers receive 800*l*." whereas they receive about 2,000*l*. It is a pity that these *errata* were allowed to remain. Vide M'Gregor, Vol. I. p. 45.

may be made for those officers and soldiers of the revolution who are yet spared as monuments of that patriotism and self-devotion, to which, under Providence, we owe our multiplied blessings."

Yet with a view to effect all these highly necessary and important objects, together with some others relating to such internal improvements as are within the control of the congress; and the whole estimated expenses of the government, an annual revenue of 15,000,000 *dollars* will suffice, or not 3,500,000*l.* The whole expenditure of the federal government will consequently hardly exceed one dollar for each individual annually throughout the union.

It must be allowed that, considering the advantages and security to individuals, found in America, and the efficient manner in which all her diplomatic, military, and other services are conducted, and that this estimate contemplates an increase in the *expenses and remunerations* in some of the departments of the government, this is an inconceivably small sum.

It is therefore with surprise we find some writers in Europe who broadly assert that the ideas entertained of the economy of the government of the United States are complete delusions, and that they are founded upon an entire ignorance of the subject. Thus the author of an article in the *Revue Britannique*, speaking of the supposed "cheap government of the United States,"—"C'est là une phrase faite, un lieu commun de notre éloquence parlémentaire, et qui, comme beaucoup d'autres, repose entièrement sur une erreur. Ce qui est fort étrange, c'est que cette phrase a été jetée dans la circulation par des hommes qui ont visité les Etats Unis, et qui entretiennent avec ceux de leurs citoyens qui viennent en Europe des rélations journalières. Elle n'en annonce pas moins une ignorance complète de ce qui s'y passe; c'est ce qu'il nous sera facile de démontrer."*

I confess that it does not appear to me *very singular* that this assertion of the cheapness of the government of the United States should be made principally by those who have had opportunities of personally examining the nature of the American system, as I fully participate (after passing some years in the United States) in that opinion. If the author means to say that it is a government suited to few other countries, it would certainly not be so

* "This has become a set phrase, a common-place of our parliamentary eloquence, and which, like many others, is founded solely on error. It is very singular that this phrase has been made current by men who have visited the United States, and who are in the habits of daily intercourse with such of their citizens as come to Europe. It betrays, nevertheless, a complete ignorance of what is passing there, which it will not be difficult for us to prove."

easy to contradict him: but as to its comparative economy, there can be little doubt that both theoretically and practically it is the cheapest government that could be established in a country of such extent, in the present day. The Quarterly Reviewer, however, expresses a very different opinion (the *Revue Britannique* coinciding throughout with that journal); and Captain Hall points out the supposed key to this alleged costliness of the government of the United States, namely, that each state having a separate government and jurisdiction, we are misled by quoting the expenditure of the federal government *alone* as the whole burden borne by the people of the United States to defray the national charges.

It is quite necessary to bear in mind the state-expenditures, in estimating the share of public charge borne by each individual in the United States, but in the tables appended to Captain Hall's Travels (Vol. III.), the nature of these expenses is completely misunderstood, as they are carried to account in gross, as charges directly borne by the population.

In the course of the following pages the statements published in the Quarterly Review, *Revue Britannique*, &c. will be examined in some detail, and it will not perhaps be difficult to show whence the errors have arisen in the estimates above alluded to.

## CHAPTER VIII.

Statements of Quarterly Review on the subject of United States examined.—Supposed insecurity of property.—Conservative elements.

In an article entitled "progress of misgovernment," which appeared in the Quarterly Review,* a summary is given of the financial arrangements of the United States. On perusing this statement I was surprised at the result which the reviewer deduces from his calculations, the data of which seem to be principally taken from the statistical tables appended to Captain Basil Hall's Travels. The writer of this article assumes, that it would be a great error to suppose that "the government of the United States is economical, and that it is, in fact, in proportion to its population, as expensive as that of Great Britain, or more so." As the whole article is redolent of party spirit, and evidently written with a view to influence public opinion on subjects connected with the great measure of reform, the passages in question should not perhaps be regarded as containing positive statistical statements

* Vide No. XCII. p. 594, Jan. 1832.

relating merely to the American financial system, but rather as the special pleading of a counsel, whose object is by no means to lay the whole case clearly and fairly before the public. Perhaps this may be thought as justifiable in political as in legal arguments.

The mistatements and singular inaccuracies contained in the article "Progress of Misgovernment" on the subject of America, are doubtless not the result of a wish to deceive the public mind with regard to the real position of that country. The whole article offers internal evidence that its author is personally and practically unacquainted with the people and country of which he speaks, and adds another to the thousand and one instances of the most erroneous inferences being drawn from data depending solely on hearsay or printed information, particularly where a favourite theory is in view, and that theory founded, of course, on conviction, but also turned to aid the arguments of party, with the unhesitating vehemence of political opposition.

With somewhat similar zeal for the dissemination of their own principles, and a corresponding want of practical acquaintance with the nature of European governments, I have heard Americans gravely wondering at the blindness of the English, or of other nations, in not adopting republican institutions and forms of government in all their extent, and not only arguing for the practicability of such adoption, but foretelling its speedy accomplishment. It is true, that in conversing with many of those who have visited this country, and even, with the better informed Americans, who never had any opportunities of judging personally of the state of things in England, I have found them as well aware of the utter unfitness and impracticability of a republican government in England as any sane Englishman.

If, however, the article in question be not put forward as an *ex parte* statement, but as expressing the *bonâ fide* opinions or the reviewer, it is difficult to conceive how so ingenious a writer can have imbibed such erroneous impressions as his statements are calculated to convey; the mystification must be laid to the account of his sources of information, the writer of this article having evidently never been in the United States; this appears at once, not only from the financial *exposé* which he gives, but more particularly from the preceding part of his paper, in which he treats incidentally of the stability of the institutions of America, and the security of property in that country. After insinuating that passing the reform bill will be the first step towards attacking "property itself in its details, if not the *principle of property* in England," he instances the United States as an example of the insecurity to property resulting from a government supported by a "*numerical majority.*"

The object of these remarks is not to discuss the merits of the reform bill; but as an illustration of any direct or indirect attack upon that measure, it seems that there could not have been a more unfortunate argument for an *opponent* of reform than this allusion to the degree of stability of property in the United States. Americans, or even those who have passed sufficient time in the United States to become practically acquainted with the nature and working of its institutions, will perhaps only smile at the predictions of a "time not being far distant when the majority shall attack the cause of property, as *at variance* with their own interests," and at the hints about a sort of agrarian law, &c., which appear in this article. But the extreme ignorance that in fact prevails in this country and in Europe generally on all that relates to the internal organization of government and society in the United States, is such as to give some currency to opinions and prognostics as totally unfounded as these, particularly when supported by such an authority as that of the Quarterly.

It will be my endeavour in the course of these remarks to point out the errors in the financial statements of the Quarterly, after first noticing some of the preliminary observations.

There is no country, he says, where "property *will* be so entirely and immediately at the mercy of those who may have, or fancy they have, an interest in assailing it, *as soon as* that body shall be sufficiently numerous to form the preponderating class in the community.

If an American were to reply to these remarks, I could suppose him doing so somewhat in the following manner:

Property is much subdivided, and in the freehold possession of an immense number of individuals in America; the moneyed institutions,—banks, both of the United States and of each particular state,—canal stock, rail-roads, public or state undertakings, and works of a like nature, as mining associations, bridge companies, steam-boats, &c., offer opportunities *for even the smallest capital* to be advantageously invested; so that the Americans of every class, profiting by these institutions, have almost all more or less a direct or prospective interest in upholding the present system of their country, and it would, in truth, be difficult to find the "*numerical majority*," which the reviewer anticipates, opposed to the principle of property.

Besides, the Quarterly subsequently points out "three great causes" for that security of property which has hitherto existed, that would seem to place the period predicted at an immense distance, viz. 1st, the "inexhaustible fund of unoccupied land," preventing the pressure of want; 2d, "the federal mechanism of its constitution, and the strict limitation of the powers of congress; and, 3d, and lastly, the continually recurring interest of the presidential and subordinate elections. There is no apparent reason why these "conservative elements" should not have their effect for many centuries to come. In other places the reviewer finds much to condemn in the two latter elements, yet allows that but for them "the constitution of the United States could scarcely have existed unharmed a year;" i. e. that without some of its most essential features it would be much less advantageous than it is, in practice; which I think that no American will be disposed to contradict. Indeed, notwithstanding the multitude of defects which the Quarterly, in many successive numbers has discovered in the constitution of the United States, not only as an object of imitation for other governments, in which he may be right, but what is very different, as *per se* bad for the Americans, he makes as complete an *amende* as any zealous republican could require, in these words :—"It is a scheme" (bad as it is!) "with which, indeed, the Americans may well be contented; for one *better fitted to their situation* it might not have been very easy, if possible, to devise." Notwithstanding this high eulogium, it is asserted in the article :—1st, that the law is opposed to large inheritances, and that laws have been made with a view to encroach on the rights of property; 2d, a general approaching division of property is hinted at; 3dly, that in spite of its advantages, the government is barely able to preserve its vitality against the destroying power (?) within itself. The "federal" or "conservative" power is almost extinct: the democratic party, i. e. the *numerical majority*, having so much increased. 4thly, that with the "inexhaustible fund of unoccupied land," the time is not far distant,—notwithstanding the "conservative" elements enumerated by the Quarterly, apparently in full vigour, and likely to continue so, and although this is the best possible sort of government for the United States,—the time is not far distant when the 10,000,000," or it might at once be 13,000,000—for "no opposition," he says above, "to the prevailing system now exists,"—will exercise despotic tyranny. It is difficult to say over whom, as the "single despot," placed, by the reviewer, in contrast with the millions, exists but as a figure of speech.

An American might fairly be justified in thus commenting upon the observations in the Quarterly.

## CHAPTER IX.

United States government well suited to the American people.—Testamentary disposition not interfered with by the laws.—Division of property.—Conservative principle of American government resides in numerical majority—Public lands.

But the reviewer will find many to agree with him in his former position, viz. "the Americans may well be content with their form of government, in conjunction with the three happy circumstances" which he enumerates, it would indeed not have been possible to devise one *better adapted to their country;* although even this is thought by him to be on the eve of dissolution. The objections which neutralize this fair assertion require some examination.

First, the law imposes* *no* restrictions on the power of devising property by testament. A man may leave all to his eldest son, or divide it as he pleases, reserving, however, the widow's dowry.

The *law* does not interfere with the possession or employment of property in any way: the late Stephen Girard,† a merchant and banker at Phila-

* The reviewer possibly thought that the French law on testaments was modelled upon that of the United States.

† See an art. in the New Monthly for April 1832, on M. Girard.

delphia, is a striking example of this. He died worth at least one million and a half or two millions sterling*. A great deal of property in houses and land, in the very heart of Philadelphia, belonged to him; and I recollect an immense square, in a fine situation for building, in that city, which remained inclosed within high paling, unoccupied and unbuilt upon, and applied to no useful purpose for years, and so remaining, I believe, until his death, a few months ago, from some whim of its proprietor, although "there chanced to be a great many neighbours around him to whom the possession of the land would have been convenient." I do not instance this as a solitary case, and might adduce† others without end to prove the complete power of accumulation and disposal of property in the hands of *any* individual; but the example of Girard is the more apposite, as he was neither a popular man in manners or habits‡,

* Report says near fifteen millions of dollars, or upwards of three millions sterling.

† At New York there is a gentleman supposed to be of equal wealth with the late Girard (also acquired solely by his own exertions), although not of the same singular habits. It would be a violation of the consideration due to private life to say more than that I allude to Mr J. Astor, known as the founder of a colony on the Colombia river.

‡ Without being miserly, he was very simple and economical in his habits. I have heard, that when he arrived in Philadelphia from France, he was in such humble circumstances that he obtained a living by selling sand and sawing wood in the streets;

nor *politically* of the *slightest* weight or importance, notwithstanding his immense wealth.

It is certain, however, that the principles and habits of the people generally are opposed to leaving the bulk of their fortune to the eldest, or to any one of their children to the exclusion of the others; and although there are exceptions, yet the rule in practice in the United States is to divide equally or nearly so, the property among all the sons and daughters; this is from choice and feeling the usage and *not by law*, excepting when a man dies *intestate*. But it must be remembered, that in a republic, without hereditary titles or honours to support, and with a wide and fair field for the exertion of talent and enterprise, this usage has not the inconvenience to individuals that Europeans generally may suppose, nor is it liable to many of the practical objections which exist to its adoption in countries like ours.

Secondly, that an agrarian law, or any thing approaching to it, is likely to become practicable or popular in the United States, or that it should even be proposed, is so extremely improbable, that one is inclined to suspect that the allusion to it is not

at the time he was between thirty and forty years of age. He used to affirm that the great difficulty in life is to amass the first forty dollars; that afterwards, a man, who is not a fool, can always grow rich. Some very munificent acts of his are on record.

made seriously. Those alone who are totally unacquainted with the state of the American community could for a moment entertain an idea of its possibility, and they have only to reflect upon a few circumstances to convince themselves of its utter want of foundation. The sub-division of old, and appropriation of new property,* going on (with few exceptions) almost *pari passu* with the increase of population, *i. e.* in the same relative proportion, extends its effects throughout the union. Also it should be remembered (and this applies to the third objection, *viz.* "that the 'vitality' of the actual government of the United States can scarcely be preserved by the 'federal or conservative' party, now '*all but* extinct,' against the prevailing system, or *democracy*"), the interests of the *numerical majority* are on the side of the prevailing system, and not opposed to its 'vitality.' The name or watch-word of a party may be 'conservative,' 'federal,' or tory, it matters little as a distinctive appellation; but if we look to the meaning of words, it may not be difficult to show that in a republic, at least in

He was, although uneducated, a man of strong natural good sense and ability, like most of those men who have amassed great wealth from low beginnings.

* By this is meant, the property or moneyed associations in the older states in contra-distinction to that in the recently settled country.

such a government as that of the United States, the 'conservative' principle is to be found on the popular side; it resides with the 'numerical majority,' opposed alike to aristocratic, despotic, or military governments, as to anarchy or disorder; and *that country* owes its strength, the vigour and the efficiency of its administration, 'its vitality,' precisely to this popular principle.

It might, on the other hand, not be difficult to maintain in arguing on the affairs of England, that this "conservative" principle may be found to reside in a very different party: in a monarchy, and where political power is vested exclusively in the aristocratic or moneyed interests, the arguments on this subject are founded on a totally different basis. But the reasoning of the "Quarterly" is on the system of the United States, to which its applicability appears more than doubtful.

It has been asserted in parliament, and elsewhere, as well as in the "Quarterly," that a "conservative" principle, analogous to that which is the supposed safeguard of our constitution, has been found in that provision* of the American constitution, in virtue

* ARTICLE V. OF CONSTITUTION OF UNITED STATES.

"The congress, whenever two-thirds of both houses shall deem it necessary, shall propose amendments to this constitution; or, on the application of the legislatures of *two-thirds* of the several of which no change is to be effected in it but by a concurrence of *two-thirds* of all the legislative bodies of the union in *demanding* such change, and the consent of *three-fourths* to its ratification; and also in the rule, by which, in certain cases, a majority of two-thirds of the senate of the United States is required for the adoption of measures of political importance. But I think on examination that this provision will be found to contain a few elements in common with the principle that is generally advocated by the "Quarterly" as being "conservative." At first sight it certainly appears that when a majority, wanting but one or two votes of the requisite two-thirds, is forced to yield to the wishes of a smaller party in the nation or senate, a modification of the oligarchical principle is perceptible; the minority, in fact, carrying their point. But let a question of great public interest arise, a question which awakens the attention, and calls forth the energies of the mass of the people in its support, and, *in a government constituted like that of America*, it will be found that the necessary majorities will never be wanting.

states, shall call a convention for proposing amendments, which, in either case, shall be valid to all intents and purposes, as part of this constitution, when ratified by the legislatures of *three-fourths* of the several states, or by conventions in *three-fourths* thereof, as the one or the other mode of ratification may be proposed by the congress," &c. &c.

It may be a conservative principle, but it is one that in effect has its foundation in the necessity of placing beyond a doubt the general assent to any measure of vital importance by the great preponderance required, and thus virtually amounts to an extension of the principle of governing in accordance to the will of the "*numerical majority.*"

Fourthly. The rapid diminution of the public lands will, in the course of time, doubtless alter materially the moral and political aspect of America. Still the closing up of this "safety-valve," as it has been called, of the constitution of the United States must, in all human probability, be remote. The Quarterly is almost justified in calling this an "inexhaustible fund." The government of the United States possesses, in round numbers, *one thousand millions* of acres of *unoccupied* land; and, making ample allowance for those parts which are unfruitful or inconvertible to useful purposes, it will be probably long before its population becomes inconveniently crowded.

Up to the present time, twenty millions of acres have been sold; about the same number has been granted by congress for education, internal improvement, &c.; and about eighty millions are in the market, i. e. surveyed, valued, &c. Some estimate may be formed, from the amount of appropriation of public lands during more than half a century, of the *ratio* which these available resources bear to the wants of an increasing population. At the rate of one million of acres every year, there will be, allowing for a progressively increasing demand, ample space and "verge enough" for speculation on the durability of American institutions, in so far as they depend upon this resource.*

* For some account of the public lands, see Chap. XVI.

## CHAPTER X.

Revue Britannique on Finances of the United States.—Letters of General Bernard and Mr F. Cooper, published by General Lafayette, containing answers to the statements of Revue Britannique.

In the month of June 1831, there appeared an article in the Revue Britannique published in Paris, on the finances of France and the United States, in which the expenses of the French and American governments were compared, in a similar spirit to that of the Quarterly. The result of this comparison was asserted to be that, notwithstanding the supposed economy of the American republic, its expenses exceeded, proportionately to its population, those of the French monarchy. As this unexpected statement was made public at a moment when the French budget was under discussion in the Chamber of Deputies, and clearly with a view to influence public opinion on so important a subject, it attracted much attention. General Lafayette, better acquainted with the real nature of the American government than any of his colleagues, and naturally more desirous, both on public grounds and from private feeling, of placing the subject in its true light than perhaps any of his countrymen, would have doubtless been well qualified to reply to the assertions of the Revue Britannique. He preferred, however, addressing two of his friends, in order to obtain such a statement as their intimate acquaintance with the financial details of the United States, and recent personal observation of them, would enable them at once to afford.

He thus elicited a counter-statement from two gentlemen, whose opportunities for forming a correct judgment on the statistics of the United States are undoubted, and whose competency in every sense, to furnish accurate information, few will be inclined to dispute. Mr F. Cooper, of New York, well known as the author of several excellent works, wrote a letter, addressed to General Lafayette, in answer to the statements of the Revue Britannique; and General Bernard, formerly Napoleon's confidential aide-de-camp (and subsequently several years in the service of the United States, until the revolution of 1830 afforded him an opportunity of returning to his native country, without compromising either the integrity of his principles, or the delicacy of his feelings), also answered General Lafayette's appeal by an able comparative statement on the budgets and financial arrangements of the American and French governments.

By taking the statements of these gentlemen as a guide, on the subject of the French national expenditure as compared with that of the United States, we also obtain data which much assist us in estimating their relative proportion to the expenses of our own government.

It is somewhat remarkable that both the writer in the Revue Britannique and the author of the article, "Progress of Misgovernment," in the Quarterly, take very nearly the same views of the financial and political systems of the United States, and (although differing in some of their details, particularly in their mode of instituting their comparisons) apparently with similar party views. In short, they wish to give such a description of what they, doubtless, conceive to be the *real* expenses of a popular government, as shall prove that the ideas generally entertained of their practical economy are little better than popular errors.

In effect, however, it appears, upon an examination of facts and details (the only way in statistical matters to get at a correct result), that it would be the grossest self-delusion to rely upon the congratulatory assurances of the Quarterly and of the Revue Britannique, as to the comparative economy of the governments of America and those of England and France. Unfortunately, neither theory nor practice, founded upon such erroneous data, can lead to good results, whether in peace or war, whether in a friendly or hostile feeling, as reliance upon them produces but a false estimate of the resources and efficiency of a powerful and rapidly increasing state. Relations with foreign governments are likely to be most judiciously regulated when their real relative positions, particularly on so vitally important a subject as finance, are well understood; at least it appears to me that no useful purpose can be served by misapprehension on this point, still less by any attempt to mystify the subject.

The writer of the article in the Revue Britannique, to which I have alluded, has ventured boldly to institute a comparison generally between the aggregate burdens borne by the French nation to defray the expenses of the state, and those which Americans support for a similar purpose: he even includes in his comparative estimate the military and naval establishments, foreign relations, and, in a word, all the items of the national budgets of the two countries.

He calculates that the annual sum of the whole of the public charges paid by each inhabitant of the United States is *thirty-five francs*, while in France it is but *thirty-one francs*.

The Quarterly Review does not attempt a general comparison between the expenses of Great Britain and those of the United States; but taking certain items of the respective national expenditures, comes to a prospective conclusion, that if the expenditures are not quite equal at present, yet when the population of the United States shall equal that of Great Britain, these items, by a *pro rato* increase, will, if *parliamentary pensions be omitted*, exceed the equivalent expenses in this country by 57,378*l.*, and *with* this item, only fall short of our expenditure by 166,365*l.* He proceeds also to estimate the expenses of the church in the two countries, and the result is, according to him, equally favourable to the economy of our ecclesiastical establishment, considered as an item of state expenditure. With regard to the administration of justice, he gives no *positive* estimate, but affirms, that there is *every reason to believe* that the "judiciary" expenditure of America *exceeds* that of England.

Captain B. Hall (from whose statistical tables, at the end of the third volume of his Travels in the United States, the Quarterly Reviewer seems to have taken almost all his positive information) makes the total aggregate amount of charge to each individual in the United States on an average of three years, 1825, 6, 7, to be 12*s.* $4\frac{3}{4}$*d.*, in which he does not include the expense of religious establishments.

On the other hand, General Bernard, after going over the statement of the Revue Britannique in some detail, comes to a conclusion that the total amount of the annual public expense to each individual in the United States (leaving out the ecclesiastical expenses, and some incidental items) is 11 francs 47 centimes, while that of each French inhabitant is 28 francs 12 centimes.

Mr Cooper, who premises that he rather exaggerates than diminishes the sum in his calculations, makes the amount of annual charge paid by each citizen of the United States 14 francs 5 centimes, including support of clergy, poor, &c.

It should be mentioned that the Revue makes out its calculations for the year 1829; that General Bernard and Mr Cooper take 1830—and that the latter gentleman speaks only of the citizen of New York, where, however, the *state* expenditure is among the highest in the whole union, and the clerical expenses probably quite the largest. Captain B. Hall's estimate, as I before mentioned, is on an average of three years, 1825, 6, 7, and the Quarterly founds its calculations principally upon the data of Captain Hall.

In endeavouring to show how such very different results are brought about by these writers, I shall have occasion to offer some remarks, which (particularly those that are suggested by the letters of General Bernard and Mr Cooper) will, I trust, assist the reader to form a judgment on the real nature of the statistics of the United States.

## CHAPTER XI.

General Bernard's remarks.—Department of state and foreign affairs.—War department.—Treasury department.—*Administration centrale,* &c.—State expenses.—Tolls and public roads.—Clergy.—Militia.—Summary.—Mean expense to each individual in France and America of public charges.—Extract from General Bernard's letter.

General Bernard observes with great truth, that in comparing the public expenditure of two such countries as France and the American union, placed under such essentially different circumstances, not only is industrious research necessary, but a perfect knowledge of their respective financial systems. But to expose the inaccuracy and exaggeration of the Revue Britannique, he thinks it unnecessary to do more than to lay before his readers some positive data, which he does in the form of an analysis of the French and American* budgets in parallel columns, with the corresponding items opposed to each other, so as to enable the reader at a glance to compare the amounts either in detail or otherwise. His valuation of the dollar is at 5 francs 25 centimes.

* Vide Appendix.

In examining the different items of the United States' budget, given by the general, it will be perceived that what is called the department of state corresponds to three departments of the French administration, viz. *Les Ministères des Affaires Etrangères, de la Justice, et de l'Interieur;* and that a deduction is made from the latter of 91,513,517 francs, appropriated to the *ponts et chausées, mines, lignes, télégraphiques*, and public works, &c.

It must also be observed that the war department of the United States includes some public works, internal improvement, and Indian affairs, which, being taken out of the calculation, make the relative expenses

| | |
|---|---|
| Ministère de la Guerre . . | 187,200,000 fr. |
| War department . . . . | 20,929,372 fr. 85 c. |

In the treasury department he includes the pensions to the officers and soldiers of the revolution, and in the *Ministère de la Finance*, the pension list of France.

The cost of the different public offices taken together (*l'administration centrale*), compared with the whole budget, is in France 1-59th, or about 1 and 7-10ths per cent; in the United States 1-53d, or about 1 and 3-10ths per cent, which difference may be regarded as null, by bearing in mind that the expenses of this central administration must diminish in its ratio to the whole budget, in proportion as the budget itself is augmented.

With regard to the post-office of the United States, it must be observed that this is not a *branch of public revenue*—it is so managed as to cover its expenses—excepting those of the general post-office establishment, clerks, &c., i. e. *l'administration centrale*, which is paid by the treasury. These expenses amount to 1-30th part of the total expense. In France they are much higher.

The expense of collecting the revenue, customs, &c. of France is about 11 per cent, that of the United States 3 and 4-10ths per cent; by taking together the expenses of administration, and those of collection of the revenue, compared with the whole budgets, we get for

France . . . . . 12 and 7-10ths per cent.
United States . . 5 and 3-10ths per cent.

Before General Bernard proceeds to examine in detail the calculations by which the author of the article in the Revue Britannique brings about a result so extraordinary in his comparative estimate of the burdens borne by an inhabitant of France and an American, viz. that the public charge of the

United States is, per head . . 35 francs.
And in France . . . . . . . 31 do.

he makes some general remarks, and says, with apparent justice, that there must be a great bias in the judgment of any one who could suppose that under the numerous favourable circumstances upon which he touches, as the geographical position of the United States, the commercial prosperity, small standing army, varied products, non-interference in the wars which have cost so much to other countries, and particularly, that with the form of its government (which he characterises as "*les belles institutions politiques qui regissent ce grand pays*"), it is difficult to understand how any impartial person could come to this extravagant conclusion. "*Pour arriver à cet étrange resultat,*" the author in the Revue asserts that the expenses of the different state legislatures taken *en masse* are equal to the federal budget. Thus:

| | Francs. |
|---|---|
| Federal budget . . . . . | 131,000,000 |
| States (according to the Revue Britannique) | 131,000,000 |
| Tolls, bridges, &c. . . . . . | 10,000,000 |
| Clergy . . . . . . . | 30,000,000 |
| Militia in time of peace . . . . | 50,000,000 |
| Total | 352,000,000 |

He divides this sum by what he supposes to be the amount of the population of 1830, i. e. 11,000,000, and thus obtains as the annual expense for each individual thirty-five francs.

The smallest error in this calculation is in the

amount of population for 1830. The census for which was, according to General Bernard, 12,856,497. This, allowing the above calculations of the author, would give twenty-seven francs thirty centimes, instead of thirty-five francs. The general points out the sources of the extraordinary errors in the calculations of the reviewer, and makes many very judicious remarks, which, however, as being chiefly made with a view to comparing the statistics of France with those of the United States, I shall only succinctly notice; and all observations on similar mistakes that have been made by the Quarterly and Captain Hall, shall be reserved until I come to examine their respective statements.

First, The state expenses are made by the Revue Britannique to amount to 131,000,000 francs, instead of which the general, by a calculation which is noticed in another chapter, produces 16,970,576 francs as the *maximum* of the aggregate state expenses of the union. Certainly a most remarkable difference.

Secondly, With respect to the tolls and turnpikes, this item might be fairly taken into consideration in a comparative estimate of the general expenditure of France and the United States, inasmuch as, there being no turnpikes in the former country, all the expense of making and repairing roads, &c. being included in the *ponts et chaussés, travaux publics*, &c., while no corresponding item is to be found in the American budget.

Under this head, Great Britain and the United States are on an equal footing; as the expenses of the roads are defrayed by turnpikes in the same manner in both countries; although from the much greater extent of steam navigation in America, less proportionately is paid by the inhabitants for the maintenance of roads in many states. In France it might also be remarked, that there are many bridges where tolls are paid, several in Paris; and that after all, the expense must be defrayed by the community, whether by a general impost, as in France, or a mere local tax, as by turnpikes and tolls. The difference is in the mode of collection, and the difficulty of course much greater in ascertaining the total amount where the latter mode is in use.

The whole extent of road on which a mail runs in the United States is computed, by General Bernard, at 41,225* leagues, of 25 to a degree. The tolls are generally high, both on roads and bridges, and this is the natural result of their having to extend over an immense territory with a compara-

* According to another more recent calculation, I find the distance run by mails to be about 115,176 miles English.

tively small population; the wages of labour being at the same time very high.

In general terms General Bernard calculates that out of the whole number of leagues (41,225) of mail road in the United States, about 4000 are subject to toll. Those upon which there are turnpikes are generally better kept in order than the other; and some idea of the cost of their construction, &c. may be formed by the circumstance, that although the tolls are very high, yet they rarely bring more than 4 per cent, and often much less, on the cost of making.

But these tolls being generally for the profit of private undertakings or companies, and constructed rather with a view to increase the value of land in particular districts, and for the advantage of commercial undertakings, than with a view to a profitable direct investment of money,—are no more looked upon in America as public charges than the canal tolls, ferries, bridges, &c. are in France and England. Besides which, sometimes the general government, as well as particular states, apply large sums to the construction and repairs of public roads, and carry the items to the federal or state budgets.

Thirdly, With regard to the clergy, General Bernard professes a complete disability to make any calculation, or comparison as to the annual expenses borne by the population of the United States. As it forms no part of the national or state expenditure, but each religious community supporting its own clergyman, the same difficulty exists as would be found in ascertaining the amount of the *incidental* emoluments of the clergy in France, beyond what is appropriated to them in the budget, "*s'il s'agissait d'ajouter le casuel aux émolumens portés au budget de l'état.*" He, therefore, altogether avoids entering on the subject, as not thinking himself competent to form any correct estimate upon it, and leaves out the ecclesiastical expenses of both countries in his calculations.

Fourthly, He proceeds to examine the militia estimates, and on all subjects connected with the military organization of America, there can be no better authority than General Bernard. By certain hypotheses and calculations, which however are very erroneous, the Revue Britannique values at fifty millions of francs the expense of the militia service of the United States, and then adds this enormous over-charge to the budgets of the union and of the states; but with singular inconsistency, or inadvertency, forgets to add the analogous expense in the French budget, viz. that of the national guards. Indeed, nothing but errors of this magnitude could have produced so false a conclusion as that while a Frenchman pays but thirty-one francs annually to the expenses of the state, an American pays thirty-five.

The organization of the American militia is precisely the same as that of the national guards in France. They have four reviews at most, annually, and no other regular military service, the circumstances of the country not requiring more. In case of invasion, the militia is no longer *local*, but it is, like the *garde nationale, mobilisée.* But the regular troops are alone subject to be sent beyond the territory of their own country. The system is identically the same as that of France.

Finally, He produces his statement of the expenses.—In the United States,

| | | Francs. | c. |
|---|---|---|---|
| Federal budget (including public debt) | . | 130,431,475 | 80 |
| State budget (borne by the tax-payers) | . | 16,970,576 | 00 |
| Total | . | 147,402,051 | 80 |

Dividing the sum by 12,856,479 (the population) he gets for the mean amount paid by each American, of public charge of every description, 11 francs 47c.

On the other hand, deducting from the French budget,

| | | Francs. |
|---|---|---|
| 1. The ecclesiastical expenses | . . . | 35,921,500 |
| 2. Reimbursements and compensations which do not strictly form part of the public charge | . | 41,939,397 |

there remains a sum of 900,074,432 francs, which divided by 32,000,000 (population of France) gives as the amount paid by each inhabitant in France, the above mentioned expenses excepted, 28 fr. 12 c. But if we take away that which goes towards the public debts, we find that the American pays annually but 6 fr. 6 c., while the Frenchman pays 20 fr. 37c. for the current expenses of the government.

The general then makes some prospective estimates of the future financial arrangements of the United States (comparing them with those of France), which it is not now necessary to detail. But to show the light in which a man of great intelligence, a soldier and a gentleman, in every way distinguished and estimable, considers the American union, after having passed many years in the country, and with the best opportunities of observing its institutions narrowly, I shall give an extract from his letter to General Lafayette. The quiet, reasonable, and argumentative tone of General Bernard will contrast strongly with the intemperate vituperation of writers, whose favourite theories and predictions on the subject of the United States, not having been as yet verified, continue to repeat statements to which every succeeding year brings additional contradictions, and the fallacy of which becomes evident upon impartial examination.

General Bernard thus concludes his letter to General Lafayette:—"But, general, while we continue to admire the excellent political institutions of the American union, and the remarkably enterprising spirit of its citizens, we must acknowledge that other causes, quite as powerful, have at the same time singularly contributed to the astonishing prosperity of this growing empire. Situated, it may be said insulated, on another continent, separated from ours by the ocean, it is in its power to remain uninfluenced by the formidable difficulties that assail us in Europe; and even these difficulties, while they lead us into such disastrous wars, produce indirectly incalculable advantages to the commerce of America. Founded at a time when a high degree of civilization had already made much progress in England, the British Colonies of North America received with their origin political institutions, the principles of which actuate at the present day the governments of the United States, whilst in Europe much time and many sacrifices will be necessary, not only to obtain those institutions which the progress of intelligence demands, but even to enable those institutions to be justly appreciated, and above all to be well understood by the mass of mankind. Finally, the population of the union is at the present scattered over a territory of almost equal extent with Europe (Russia, Sweden and Turkey excepted); and in this immense and rich dominion, that multiplicity of custom-houses, and fiscal internal demarcations, which so much injure and clog the development of European industry, are not to be found. Europe is without doubt the finest portion of the world, the part which, on an equal given space or superficies, presents the most abundant resources of every kind; but instead of mutually contributing to a common prosperity, the nations of Europe, actuated by rivalries without end, pour out their blood and exhaust their treasure to destroy each other, and mutually paralyse their progress towards a better system. What a lesson for the American union! when once this is destroyed, its ruins would soon fall into the same labyrinth of difficulties as at this moment disturbs and perplexes the nations of Europe."

## CHAPTER XII.

Capt. Hall's estimate of mean charge to each inhabitant of the United States.—Mr F. Cooper's remarks on the Revue Britannique.—Mr Cooper's estimate of mean public charge.

CAPTAIN B. HALL makes the total amount of what each person pays to the state and general governments, on an average of three years, 1825-6-7, to be 12*s.* 4¾*d.*, which is much nearer the truth, it appears to me, than either the calculations of the Revue Britannique or those of the Quarterly. Indeed, differing from that gentleman *toto cœlo* as I do, in the impressions received from a residence in the United States (of much longer duration than Captain Hall's), and however different my opinions of the future prospects of that rising and interesting country connected with its present form of government, I cannot forbear to give my humble testimony in favour of the general accuracy of all the statements of that gentleman that bear upon matters of fact and local description;—do not let me be misunderstood, as supposing that it can be necessary to vindicate Captain Hall in this country, or perhaps even in America, from a charge of intentional misrepresentation.

The reviews and journals of that country do not generally accuse him of this: on the contrary, many of the extracts which are given by American writers sufficiently show that he in a thousand instances did justice to what he saw there; but it has been asserted that a strong political bias—a powerful feeling of prejudice—continually interfered with the exercise of his judgment when drawing inferences from what he saw, and making general and not laudatory reflections upon that which he had just before been describing with warm approbation.*

The sum calculated by Captain Hall, like that of General Bernard, leaves out the expenses of the church and the public turnpike roads; the error in its amount will be easily accounted for in examining the calculations of Mr Cooper and those of the Quarterly.

Mr Fenimore Cooper had been requested by General Lafayette to rectify errors in the statements of the Revue Britannique; the general thus explains his object in requesting Mr Cooper to undertake a task for which he is so eminently qualified. "Independently of our common American interest on this subject, I feel a wish to undeceive

* Vide Review of Captain B. Hall's Travels in North America, 2d ed. London, published by Kennett, &c.

such of my French colleagues as may conscientiously believe that they ought to oppose reductions in the expenditure, from the erroneous impression that the taxes of this country (France) are less oppressive than the combined expenses of the federal and state governments of the union."

Mr Cooper, after some general observations, remarkable for their fairness and the judgment with which he notices some of the sources of error in the theories and reasonings that are frequently applied to the affairs of America, and regretting that he has not at hand the materials and authorities that he could wish, proceeds to give an outline of the origin and state of the national debt of the United States, part of which will be found in the Appendix.*

Before examining farther Mr Cooper's statement, it is necessary to give the extract from the Revue Britannique, which gave occasion for it.—" The federal budget of the United States, which might also be called their political budget, did not exceed, in 1829, 24,767,119 dollars (or 131,265,729 francs), but in time of war† it amounts to more than twice that sum."

* Vide Appendix at the end of the volume.

† In the original it is " mais en tems de *paix*, il s'elève à plus du double," evidently a misprint.

"Doubtless the moderation of this budget will strike one forcibly when compared with the enormous amount of ours. We are inclined to envy the fortunate position of a nation freed from the diversity of our fiscal imposts, and which in fact has, it may be said, but a single source of revenue, that of the customs. It will be calculated that even were our army reduced to a low peace establishment, our budget would still amount to near a thousand millions. The result would be, that in France the mean amount of the public charge paid by each individual is 31 francs, whilst in the United States it is but 13 francs:—but this is a mere deception. It must be borne in mind that the twenty-four states composing the American union, are not provinces or departments, but independent states, having each their separate budget, as they also have a separate constitution. To ascertain, therefore, the public expenditure of the United States, it becomes necessary to add the particular budgets of every state to the federal budget, which only embraces the collective expenses of the union. One must also place to account the different county expenses which are not quoted either in the general or state budgets: add to this the expenses of making and repairing roads, as on none of our roads are any tolls levied, but this item is included in the national budget. In the United

States, on the other hand, a great number of the roads are turnpike roads, on which a toll is paid by all who use them. One must, therefore, if the amount of these tolls were ascertained, add it to the other public expenses. Before we proceed to examine the state budget, let us analyse some items of the federal budget, and we shall find, that the salaries which are paid out of it, far from being subjected to a rigorous economy, are almost in every case higher than those paid for the corresponding services in France."

"The political communities, which have lately been reconstructed in Europe upon a new basis, have all deemed it indispensable for the maintenance of tranquillity, to place a sovereign in the highest place in their social hierarchy. They have necessarily been obliged to burden themselves with a considerable expense, to invest the family in which the superior power is made hereditary with the requisite splendour. The genius of America, having in some sort sufficient space in which to employ its glowing spirit of enterprise, does not appear to have as yet required this condition to avoid turbulence and disquiet. There are forest regions to clear, savage tribes to subdue, immense, innumerable plains to be cultivated: no expense, therefore, equivalent to what we denominate civil list, is to be found in the federal budget, although there is one item nominally the same, but which represents expenses of a different nature. As has been already said, a constitutional king, none of whose acts are voted without the countersign of a responsible minister, reigns, but does not govern. The President of the United States, who does govern, has no counterpart in France, but the President of the council, placed like him at the head of affairs: his emoluments are 25,000 dollars (or 132,500* fr.). The president of the council in France is fixed at 120,000 francs in the national budget. The President of the United States has, besides, a magnificent hotel in Washington, and a country villa† in the neighbourhood of that town. Notwithstanding this, it appears that his appointments are insufficient to cover the expenses to which, by usage, he is subjected. One of these expensive customs is, the necessity of giving, during the session of congress, two grand dinners, which are far from being remarkable for that simplicity attributed by us to republican manners: these dinner-parties, and the other expenses incident to the representation kept

* 132,500, or between 5 and 6000*l.*

† This is not the case: the mistake probably arose from the accidental circumstance of the family of the late President (Mr Adams) occupying at one time a country-house very near Washington.

up by the President, deranged the fortunes of many of those who have filled the post of supreme magistrate. Mr Jefferson and Mr Munroe died, it may be said, almost insolvent."

I believe that Captain Hall was the first writer on the United States who called public attention in Europe to the duplicate form of government of the American union, and pointed out the necessity of taking into any calculation of the whole expenditure of that country, the *general* and state budgets to which each inhabitant of the United States contributes. The errors in his calculations are in the *amount* which he allows for their joint sums; and although he comes much nearer the truth than either the Quarterly or the Revue Britannique, he evidently does not take into consideration many circumstances the ignorance of which has also misled the authors of the articles in the above-mentioned journals.

The amount of annual charge paid by each individual in the United States is made by Mr Cooper (valuing the dollar at 5 francs 33 centimes) to amount to 14 francs 5 centimes. This sum does not materially differ from that given by Captain Hall (viz. 12*s.* 4¾*d.*); but there is this important difference in their calculations; Mr Cooper includes in his estimate, not only the federal and the state budgets, but the expense of *public schools*, of the *clergy*, the *poor*, and every *incidental expense;* whereas Captain Hall only reckons the combined expenditure of the general and state governments. For the *two budgets alone*, Mr Cooper calculates the mean charge per head at 10 francs 40 centimes, or about one franc less than General Bernard's estimate* (11 francs 47 centimes), which also omitted the clergy. Before I proceed to examine in detail how these different results have been produced, the estimates of the Quarterly should be taken into consideration ; as, although not given in the same form as those which have been already mentioned, they will in fact be answered in the course of the examination of the others.

* It must also be recollected that General Bernard calculates the dollar at 5 francs 25 centimes, while Mr Cooper reckons it at 5 francs 33 centimes.

## CHAPTER XIII.

Quarterly's remarks on American statistics.—General and state expenditure.—General Bernard's and Mr Cooper's estimates.

After some preliminary remarks, the writer of the article, "Progress of Misgovernment," observes, that "we are not to infer that there is no unnecessary expenditure under the American system," and that in fact those establishments which they have in common with us are not "on a much *more economical scale* than our own." He differs from the Revue Britannique, inasmuch as he says, "It is true that the salary and establishment of the President are framed on a scale of *severe republican simplicity*." "But," he adds, "on the other hand, be it remembered, there are certain other civil disbursements, in the shape of salaries, from which our monarchical establishment is exempt. Be it remembered that, besides the two houses of congress, there are twenty-four local houses of representatives and twenty-four senates* continually in existence,

* This is not precisely the case: in Vermont, for instance, there is no senate, and the upper house in New Jersey is styled the "legislative council;" but this is immaterial to the general argument.

and during a considerable portion of the year in actual session, in the several states, &c. &c., and that every one of these delegates is paid,—those serving in the general congress receiving as much as eight dollars, or about 1*l.* 16*s.* per day, during the session, besides a like sum for every twenty miles of distance from his residence to the seat of congress." In all this information the reviewer is generally right, as well as in all the other facts taken from the tables appended to Captain Hall's Travels.*

But his mode is quite different of bringing forward his proofs of the assertion in the former part of his remarks, viz. that the expenses of the gov-

* The manner in which his subsequent calculations are made, reminds one of that part of Captain Hall's Travels, where a characteristic conversation is given between a shrewd old Irish settler and a land agent:—on asking the old emigrant for information about the settlement, he began to suspect some lurking motive in these, as he thought, leading questions—"What shall I say to the gentleman, sir?"—"Why, Cornelius, said the agent, "tell the truth." "O yes, of course, sir, we must always tell the truth, but—*if I only knew what the gentleman wanted, I would know which way to answer*—in short, should I *overstate* matters, sir, or should I *understate* them? shall I make things *appear better or worse than they are?*"

It may possibly be recollected by more than one member of our own legislature, that there were modes some years ago of making out parliamentary calculations, very much upon the principle of the Irish emigrant;—at least, such things have been asserted,—and the calculations of the Quarterly remind one strongly of this sort of over and under statement.

ernment under the American system nearly equal those of Great Britain. He does not calculate the mean amount of public charge borne by each individual, the mode adopted by Captain Hall, the Revue Britannique, Mr Cooper, and General Bernard, but taking certain parts of the American expenditure, compares their gross amount with the corresponding items in the English budget. He thus obtains 624,538*l.* for the entire civil expenditure of the American republic (which we shall not at present analyse, but allow for the sake of argument to be correct). He then turns to statements laid before parliament, and finds that our civil list, salaries and allowances paid out of the consolidated fund, our courts of justice, amount to 1,269,765*l.* But as he says, "these are expenses which ought necessarily to bear a direct proportion to population, if not to wealth;" and the population of Great Britain and Ireland being about 24,110,125, he, by assuming that *the expenditure of the union* shall increase *pro rato* with its population, it follows, that when it shall have attained twenty-four millions, "the expenditure will be fifty-seven thousand pounds more than ours!"

To obtain this singular result, it is true, as the Quarterly observes, he has indeed left out "the parliamentary pensions and annuities, granted for the most part in consideration of eminent public services"—because, forsooth, there is no corresponding item *in this department* of the American accounts: this omission, which many people might be inclined to think not wholly unimportant in a comparative estimate of the expenditure of the two governments, is subsequently rectified by taking the amount of the revolutionary pensions in the United States, and by setting them off against the parliamentary pensions, he still gets a balance in favour of America of no more than 166,365*l.*

In the first place it must be remarked, that the Quarterly, in common with Captain B. Hall, and the writer in the Revue Britannique, is wrong with respect to the amount of the state expenditure, and in consequence all their calculations are wide of the truth; allowing that the mean, taken from the tables of Captain Hall, is correct as applied generally (and it is far from being so, by reason of the preponderance of the richer and more populous states in the calculation), it seems to have been quite forgotten, that a very small part of this nominal amount is *really a charge upon the tax prayers.* In almost every state a considerable share of the expenditure is covered by the interest of different funds; in many, a large portion of the state budget is appropriated to internal improvements, which become in their turn sources of public revenue.* Such are the great canals of New York, Pennsylvania, Ohio, &c. By making the requisite deductions, according to the best information that I have been able to obtain, from the sums paid throughout the union to the support of the state expenses, I think that something more than one shilling sterling (instead of three shillings, according to Captain Hall and the Quarterly) is about the amount of the mean charge for state expenditure. But this amount cannot, without possessing more local information than most foreigners can obtain, and devoting much time to the subject, be given with any accuracy. It will be probably better therefore to take the calculations of General Bernard and Mr Cooper as our guide on this head. General Bernard takes an average of the expenditure of two of the richest and most populous states of the union, viz. New York and Virginia, and thus obtains one franc 32 centimes as the maximum per individual of annual charge. By not being aware of the real

* Thus in Pennsylvania, for instance, nearly two millions and a half are given as the state expenditure; but it should be observed, that at the time that Captain Hall alludes to, some millions had been employed, in the course of two or three years, by that state, for making a canal, afterwards to become a profitable source of revenue to the state itself; and consequently the two millions and upwards were far from being the true amount of the usual state expenditure, and so of other states.

nature of the state budget, the Revue Britannique, as well as Captain Hall, and the Quarterly, have given totally false estimates of the amount of the state expenses. Thus the Revue Britannique, whose calculations are principally made from the budget of New York, reckons the state expenditure at 10,179,498 francs, whereas, there is out of this sum no more than 1,837,500 francs paid by the inhabitants of that state. The remainder is paid by the interests of the funds belonging to the state, and by the receipts of the Erie and Champlain canals, which latter alone amount to near 5,000,000 francs.

Mr Cooper, himself a citizen of New York, and of course more likely to be intimately acquainted with the details of the expenditure of this state than a foreigner, makes the mean annual charge of each inhabitant of New York to be 95 centimes, or within one sous of a franc; and he thinks that this is a fair criterion for the amount of the rest of the union. He takes the average real expenditure for five years, and estimates it at 350,000 dollars. This amount seems very small; but it must be recollected that although each state is considered as a separate and independent government, yet none but the federal government has to defray the expenses of any regular armed force; that they have no naval department, and no foreign relations, to keep up. It must also be borne in mind, that the large and increasing revenue of the canals, salt works, &c. in proportion as the mortgages upon the revenues will be paid off, will become available in a greater proportion by the state, so that upon a moderate valuation, when quite unincumbered, the canals, salt works, &c. will produce a revenue, in Mr Cooper's opinion, four times greater than the sum required for the expenses of the state. It should also be recollected, that in comparing the amount of expenditure in the two countries, we should take into account the poor-rates, county-rates, &c. in England, which will be found, at a very moderate computation, much to exceed the aggregate of the state expenses of America.

## CHAPTER XIV.

Future financial prospects of the United States.—Military expenses.—Naval expenses.—Cost of administration of justice.—Salaries of the clergy.

THE calculation in the Quarterly that when the population of the United States shall equal our own, the expenditure will be proportionally increased, is not likely to prove correct either in theory or practice. The immense extent of territory in the United States, the scattered position of many of its inhabitants, and the nature of its border and southern population, require a vast framework of organization both for military and judicial purposes, and an apparently disproportionate expense; thus the skeletons of the regiments composing their small army are made upon a scale that would admit of a considerable augmentation with a trifling increase of expense, as the staff and officers, as well as the number of clerks employed in the war office, and the other parts of the military organization are kept up on a footing that would allow of a great increase of effective force with little addition to the budget, beyond the pay of the additional privates. On this head the opinion of General Bernard, who for several years filled a high military post in the service of the United States, is of much weight; he says, "that the American army might be increased to 12,000 men (or about double its present number) without any sensible augmentation in the expenses of the war department at Washington (*l'administration centrale*). That the number of privates is reduced as low as possible, while the officers are kept up on a scale adapted for thrice the effective numerical force; by which means the general expenses are diminished in time of peace, and they are prepared with a sufficient number of officers on the breaking out of war."

It may be remarked, that the expenses of the military force of the United States, when compared with those of many of the European armies, are disproportionately great, amounting for about 6,000 men to nearly 21 millions of francs, or about 4,200,000 dollars. It should be recollected that the American soldier is enrolled by voluntary enlistment, and the wages of labour in the United States being very high, he will of course expect a proportionate remuneration for his services. Besides, a sum of 525,000 francs, annually voted for the manufacture of musquets and small arms, is included in the above estimate, as also the expenses of a formidable line of fortifications now in progress, with its artillery and that of the army.* In like manner the expenses of the navy department at Washington would not materially increase if it became necessary to put twice the present number of ships of war in commission.

The same necessity exists for a large proportionate expense to the federal government in the administration of justice, the framework of which is at present calculated rather upon the extent of territory than upon the number of inhabitants, as the organization is uniform and general. On this subject Mr Cooper thus expresses himself, "The maintenance of order, and the administration of justice, would not cost much more, were the population 100 millions, than they do at present for less than 14 millions. No person is allowed to hold more than one place or office, and none of those now employed could be dispensed with without detriment to the public service. It is necessary to support thirty district courts for a population of less than 14 millions, whereas, if the union were of no greater extent than France, proportionally

* These fortifications have been carried on, and, in many instances completed, under the able superintendence of General Bernard.

to its number of inhabitants, four courts would suffice."

Allowing for a very natural bias in favour of the institutions of his country, it may be probable that Mr Cooper has overrated the economy of the administration of justice; still his observations deserve much consideration.

There is also a charge peculiar to the United States,* which is the sum paid to the Indian tribes, and this alone amounts to about one-twentieth of the whole American budget, and is not likely to increase in the same ratio as the population of the country.

But the errors and misconceptions on all that relates to the statistics of the United States in this article of the Quarterly, are nowhere more conspicuous than in that part where the annual expense of the clergy is estimated. The reviewer founds his calculations upon the statement of Dr Cooper,† from which he estimates the aggregate amount paid throughout the union to the clergy *of all sects* at £3,081,650;‡ and as on the same

* The government of our North American colonies have a similar item in their expenditure.

† Dr Cooper is, or was, professor at one of the colleges in the United States,* and is, I believe, no relation of Mr F. Cooper.

‡ The Revue Britannique, not wishing to understate, gives as

* Columbia, South Carolina.

authority he states the number of clergymen to be about 13,000, he obtains 237*l.* 10*s.* as the average annual stipend of each clergyman (1000 dollars, according to Dr Cooper), exclusive of occasional emoluments ("irregular exactions and fees," &c.). This he contrasts with the sum of the tithes in the hands of the clergy "in England, which," he says, "from very satisfactory evidence, does not much exceed £2,215,000;" and that, "*if the tithes were equally divided among all the livings*," each clergyman would have but £200; that by adding the cathedral property, and the income of the bishops, you cannot establish an aggregate of more than £2,673,500.

If the accuracy of this statement could be admitted, it would at once do away with an objection that has been sometimes made to the church system in the United States, viz.—that unless the provision for the church were compulsory, and its support established by law, the clergy would starve. But, although I can fully bear witness, as far as my observation goes, to the fact that the clergy of the Episcopalian and some other forms of worship in America are not only respectably maintained, but that they, in fact (whatever may be their nom-

the revenue of the clergy in America 30,000,000 francs, or about £1,200,000.

inal income, or the comparative cheapness of their place of residence), live in comfort and competence, and that I never either saw or heard of clergymen being in want or distressed, so as not to be able to support and provide for their families with more than the mere necessaries of life; yet the rate calculated by the reviewer is much too high. It is extremely difficult to form an accurate estimate of either the number of the clergy in the United States or the amount of their emoluments. If one were required in this country to make out an exact schedule of the income enjoyed by the clergy of the established church, notwithstanding the assistance afforded by the *Liber Regalis* and the clerical guide, it would not be easy to get the precise amount of the *real* income of the clergy, including cathedral property, Easter offerings, glebes, oblations, dues, pews in the church, fees, &c. &c. A proof of the difficulty of obtaining a true estimate may be found in the various sums at which the revenues of the Anglican church have been valued. The Quarterly says £2,673,500 in one place, and £3,872,138 in another.* But other valuations certainly have been made, and many published in the various London journals, which vary from four to even nine millions and

* Vide Vol. XXIX. of Quarterly Review, p. 555.

more. As it is no part of the object of this work to examine into the real amount of the temporalities of the church of England, but to show what is the probable sum of the income of the clergy in the United States, I shall not take any other valuation than that of the Quarterly Reviewer, certainly not likely, from the tenor of his argument, to be exaggerated.

## CHAPTER XV.

Ecclesiastical revenues of the United States.—Valuations of the Quarterly of church of England revenues, and those of the clergy of America.—Probable *real* amount of church emoluments in the United States.

But if it be not easy to form a correct estimation of the revenue of the church of England, what must be the difficulty of getting at the true value of all the sums appropriated throughout Great Britain and Ireland to the support of the clergy of *all denominations?* In Scotland it would be comparatively easy, and in Ireland, as far as the legally established church is concerned; but, to put the question on fair grounds, we must include not only the Catholic clergy of Ireland, but the Presbyterians, and all the dissenters of the united kingdom. The reviewer admits this, with regard to the dissenters, in speaking of *England* only, and allows that it might be more than sufficient to make up the difference between his *estimate* of the relative amounts of the incomes of each clergyman in the two countries, i. e. between 2,673,500*l.** in Eng-

* This is the estimate in the 92d vol. of the Quarterly; that in the 29th being above a million more.

land and 3,081,650*l.* in the United States. It must be remembered, also, that in this comparative estimate the church of Ireland, that is to say, the established church, is not included, nor is Scotland taken into account; whereas, in the calculation of 13,000 clergymen in the United States, *all denominations* are included in *all parts* of that extensive country.

Thus allowing the correctness of the above estimate, the annual income of the church, or rather of the clergy, in the United States would at once appear to be infinitely below that of the clergy of the united kingdom; and this is to be expected as a matter of course, from the totally different circumstances of the church in the two countries. In America the clergy have no connexion with the government, or with any political party, directly or indirectly; they are not magistrates, nor do they take part in any of the lighter recreations of society that in this country are looked upon as at least harmless amusements. Clergymen are rarely, if ever, seen either at a ball or party; nor do they mix much in general and large companies, unless when brought together for the promotion of some charitable measure, or some association connected with their religious duties. It is not intended to institute a comparison between the habits and principles of the American clergy and those of the church of England, but to mention facts that account for their total difference of position in social and political life. Indeed, the difference of feeling in the two countries is so great, that if a clergyman were, in most parts of the United States, to be seen at a theatre, at a dance, or to join a card party, he would certainly fall in the esteem and opinion of his flock; but if he were to become habitually a frequenter of balls, plays, &c. or be tempted to become a sportsman or fox-hunter, he certainly would not long continue to fill the station of pastor to any congregation. I do not pretend to give any opinion as to the comparative merits of the two systems, nor is either censure or approbation implied of the severity of public opinion in America on this subject. These facts, however, joined to the absence of all political or worldly dignities in the ecclesiastical body in the United States, render large incomes quite unnecessary to the clergy of that country; and the assertion, therefore, of the mean amount of their emoluments being greater than, or nearly equal to, that of the clergymen of England, is the more surprising.

On examination, however, I think that there will be found little reason to suppose this to be the case. The Quarterly takes Dr Cooper's estimate as its guide, and thus finds that the aggregate of the salaries of the clergy in the United States is 3,081,650*l.* inasmuch as there are 13,000 clergymen at 1000 dollars, or 237*l.* 10*s.* each. But this valuation is so extremely exaggerated in its amount, that one is at a loss to conceive how it can have been made from any authentic data. The Revue Britannique, judging by Williams's Register, published at New York, and one of the best authorities for that city of the salaries of the clergy, makes the whole amount of clerical income in the United States about 1,200,000*l.*, which, although less than half the sum given by the Quarterly, is still probably much more than the real amount, as in many parts of the union the expenses of the clergy by no means equal those in the state of New York.

But to enable those who are unacquainted with the ecclesiastical affairs of America to form an opinion on this question, it will be necessary to mention a few circumstances peculiar to the clergy of the United States.

With respect to the ministers of religion, no legislative provision is made in any of the states, or by the general government, for their support. It is left entirely to the voluntary acts of individuals, and the good-will of the congregations of the different sects and denominations; excepting, however, that in the state of Massachusetts, the constitution compels all citizens to belong to some religious society, or to pay for the support of some religious teacher, leaving them to contribute to whatever society or denomination they may choose.

From a list of the ministers of different denominations to be found in the Appendix, it appears that the number of clergymen is 10,120; by another enumeration they are made to amount to no more than 8520. But let us avoid the possibility of underrating the number of ministers of religion paid by the people of the United States, including the licentiates as well as the ministers. It must also be recollected that among the methodists there are many whose ministers are not allowed to reside more than two years in any one place, and part of whose church discipline it is to be continually travelling and preaching in all parts of the union, indeed it may be said in all parts of the world, for from some of these I believe are generally taken the missionaries who proceed to the islands of the Pacific, to New Zealand, &c. to preach the Gospel. The extreme difficulty, therefore, of coming to any very accurate estimate of their number is apparent. These ministers receive *in money* but about sixty dollars, or about 12*l.* or 13*l.* annually, if unmarried, or about twice that sum when married, and therefore practice very literally the scriptural injunction —"Lay not up for yourselves treasure upon earth;" but it is true that their support is not wholly provided for by this stipend, as during their progress through the country they are generally received into the families of some of those belonging to their congregations, among whom are always found persons able and willing to exercise their hospitality towards the clergy of their church. There is a hierarchy of this denomination, and there are others who are not Episcopalians.

In 1830 there were in New York 1382 clergymen, according to Williams's Register; of these, there was, perhaps, not one whose annual income would exceed 1000*l.*, few with more than 500*l.*; and I should think, from all the authorities that I have been able to consult, that 100*l.* per annum would be rather more than the average salary of each clergyman; and in that state the clergy are probably paid higher than in any other. It is difficult to ascertain with certainty the existence of a greater number of clergymen than from 8500 to 10,100, throughout the union;—but allow it to be 10,200, or even 11,000 (and this amount will certainly be more than can be proved), and we obtain 1,100,000*l.* as the total amount of church income in America; and this, I think, is much more than the true sum.

Possibly Dr Cooper reckons the preachers of those sects, among whom there is no regular clergy, but where one of the congregation occasionally officiates, although possibly a mechanic or farmer, or person engaged in any other employment or trade; of whom there are, I believe, many in Great Britain; —but it should be recollected that these men receive no salary as clergymen, and therefore cannot be included in the estimate.

But Mr F. Cooper makes a lower calculation than that given above. His remarks on this subject deserve attention. In speaking of the clergy of New York, he says, "Their emoluments are derived from two sources, the revenues belonging to certain churches, and voluntary contributions. The greater portion of the higher stipends (I allude to those amounting to from eight to twenty thousand francs, and their number is very limited), are the proceeds of estates or property enjoyed by the clergymen, or arise from the rent of pews and sittings in the places of worship; the smaller salaries are paid by means of subscriptions raised for that object. According to Williams, there were in 1830 in New York 1382 ecclesiastics, having each their church. *We should much exceed the real amount*, if we allow that each of these *receives on the average* 400 dollars, or about eighty to eighty-five pounds. Of the whole number 400 are methodists, who do not receive, as I know from good authority, more than 300 dollars; and 600 dollars are considered a very good salary in a country of some importance. I recollect that the principal minister of Cooperstown, which is the capital of a county, received but the latter sum, which was defrayed solely by the rent of seats. Therefore, in allowing 400 dollars as the salary of an ecclesiastic in New York, we are above the real average. He goes on to say—"Funerals cost nothing; prayers for the living or the dead are gratuitous; the same is the case for baptisms and marriages. Any priest who *should refuse to perform any of these duties without payment, would run a great risk of losing his living*. It is the custom to make an offering to the priest who has performed the marriage ceremony, but it is quite voluntary. And a small number of wealthy people make presents also on the occurrence of a christening or baptism; but the greater number of Americans regard donations on such occasions with a religious horror. They consider it as an attempt to corrupt Heaven. In town, gloves and scarfs are given to the priests, as well as to the physicians and the bearers, by a few families, at funeral ceremonies; but we are so far from thinking it necessary to pay an ecclesiastic for a funeral, that for my own part, although accustomed to the habits of other countries, *I retain for this practice a feeling of profound aversion.* In a word, a priest in America is considered as a minister of God. He is paid that he may exist; but no one is of opinion that those *who do not pay him have less right to his ministry than those who do.*"*

It will be seen from the foregoing extract from Mr Cooper's Letter, that he estimates the ecclesiastical expenses at about one fifth lower than I have reckoned them (1,100,000*l.*); but even allowing the higher valuation, there is a difference of nearly two millions sterling in the amount, as given by the Quarterly. The reviewer's valuation of the amount of the ecclesiastical revenue in England has nothing to do with the present object, which is not to institute a comparison between the English and American church revenue. But it must be evident that, judging by the returns for the county of Lancaster, which have been published, it seems inconceivably below the real amount. The amount of church property *in the hands of churchmen* in that county alone greatly exceeding the whole sum

I regret that I cannnot give Mr Cooper's own words, as it is only from the French published translation of that gentleman's letter that the above citation is made, and it is very probable that justice is not done to the style of that author in my re-translation.

allowed by him for the cathedral property of all England.

The gross amount of the property for the county of Lancaster is upwards of three millions per annum; and it is perhaps not one of the least objections to the church system in England, that a great part of the large sums nominally paid for its support, are, in fact, nothing more than a species of lay property, often passing from hand to hand, and unconnected with any benefit to the ministry of religion, excepting that the *onus* (and it may be added *odium*, with at least the unreflecting and uninformed* part of the community) of levying and realizing the sums, falls to the share of the church.

From what has been shown, then, it will be clear that we rather overrate the account of church revenues in the United States by estimating them at £1,100,000; while, if we take the whole income

* There can be no greater proof of the difficulty of obtaining a true estimate of the income of the clergy of the church of England than the valuations to be found in the Quarterly itself. Let us take but two instances. In the article "Progress of Misgovernment," No. 92, we find the church revenues calculated at about £200 per annum for each clergyman, and an aggregate, with cathedral property, of £2,673,500. But, referring to No. 58 (Vol. XXIX. p. 556, *et seq.*), we find the total revenue of the established church £3,872,138! and that of the parochial clergy £3,447,138, or, for each clergyman, £303 annually. While in the church of Scotland each living is valued at £275, and the aggregate £263,340.

of the established church of Great Britain and Ireland, the support of the clergy in Scotland, and that of the Roman catholics, and of all the various sects of dissenters throughout the United Kingdom, £12,000,000 will be a very low valuation.

This is the only fair mode of comparing the ecclesiastical expenditure of the two countries.*

* Much has been said lately about a "free trade in religion." If this phrase have any meaning as applied to the United States, I am at a loss to discover it. There are few countries where there is less of trade or pecuniary considerations in connexion with the ministers of religion than America. Livings can neither be bought nor sold, nor money received on account of the church, but by individuals performing certain duties, for which, in the opinion of those who benefit by their ministry, they are supposed most eligible. It would be a great mistake to suppose that even the mere external demonstrations of deep respect for religious ordinances are not observable in most parts of the United States. In a great many states there is annually a fast day proclaimed by the governor of the state, and its observance neither meets with the animadversion, nor the opposition that similar proclamations have been met with in this country. The general respect for the ordinances of the Sabbath is also at least as great (except, I am informed, in the southern extremity of the union) as in any country with which I am acquainted.

## CHAPTER XVI.

Expenses of administration of justice.—Of state judiciaries.—Some account of public lands, and future intentions with regard to them.

WITH respect to the expenses of the administration of justice, called in the United States "the judiciary," the Quarterly speaks only in general terms, but asserts that to the country at large it is probably more costly than "to any other in the world!" acknowledging, however, that he knows of no data sufficiently accurate from which to state the proportions which the expenses of this department bear to each other in the two countries respectively; at least not with the "*same precision*" as in the cases of the civil and ecclesiastical department.

In the Appendix will be found a table which may assist in forming an estimate of the amount of the expenses of the *state* "judiciaries," in which are included the salaries of chief justice, judges, attorneys and solicitors-general, reporters, municipal-courts, police-courts, &c. as complete as it has been in my power to make it at present, by which it appears that the average annual expense to the country for the state judiciary is about 395,866 dollars. If we allow 90,000*l.* for this item, it will certainly not be underrating it.

Although the magistrates are paid by fees, yet they are so low, that we may very safely estimate the usual fees of clerks of the peace and petty law-officers in this country, as being more than equivalent to them.

The principal sources of revenue in the United States, are the imports, the public lands, and bank dividends. But the first named alone will be sufficient to meet all the expenditure, even after the sale of bank-stock proposed by the present secretary of the treasury, and without the sums hitherto derived from the sale of public lands.

Among the less prominent sources of revenue of the United States, there are some that deserve notice from their daily increasing importance, if not from their present value. The gold mines, the sugar plantations, the cultivation of vineyards, and the production of silk manufactures, &c. are worthy of attention in forming an estimate of the financial prospects of the United States.

The public lands were very early looked to as a source of revenue to the country. As early as 1776, Silas Deane, then a political and commercial agent of the United States in France, communicated to congress a plan for the sale and settlement of the territory north-west of the Ohio; and, as has been already observed, the calculations of the future value of this region formed the first great subject of collision between the several states of the confederacy. It was, however, a long time before an effective system was devised, by which the lands could be thrown open to settlement, or made available for the purpose of revenue.

Bounty-lands having been promised by the continental congress to the officers and soldiers of the continental army, it became necessary to redeem that pledge as early as possible. The controversies between the several states, and between them and the United States, retarded for some time the fulfilment of this pledge. On the 20th May 1785, an ordinance was passed by the congress of the confederation, for ascertaining the mode of disposing of lands in the western territory, and this was the first act of general legislation on the subject. This act may be found in the new edition of the Land Laws, page 349. Under it very limited sales were made, not amounting, in the whole, to more than 121,540 acres.

Subsequently different sales were effected in proportion as lands were ceded to the United States by any of the individual states. Pennsylvania became a purchaser, and the Ohio Land Company also became large buyers to the amount of two millions of acres, afterwards reduced by agreement to one million; they paid two-thirds of a dollar per acre. This company originated in Massachusetts, and commenced the settlement of Ohio (then an uninhabited wilderness) in 1788; it now supports a population of about 1,000,000. Another sale was effected by an individual, named J. Symmes, of between 2 and 300,000 acres. He succeeded perfectly in settling the territory north-west of the Ohio.

But it was not till 1802 that the many and troublesome controversies that took place between the general government and the different states on the subject of the public lands were amicably adjusted.

North Carolina ceded to the United States the tract of country now forming the state of Tennessee, in 1789; and Georgia, after much embarrassing discussion, was the last to enter into the arrangement with the United States, by ceding that territory, now forming the states of Alabama and Mississippi; the United States contracting to extinguish the Indian title to lands within the limits of Georgia, "as soon as it could be done peaceably, and on reasonable terms."

Some account of the mode in which the public lands are disposed of in the United States may not be uninteresting at a moment when emigration is hourly increasing to our American colonies and the United States.

On the 10th of May 1800, an act of congress was passed, laying the foundation of the land system as it now exists. It has received several modifications at subsequent periods, two of which are of great importance, and will presently be stated.

Under this law, the substantial features of the land system of the United States are the following:

All the lands, before they are offered for sale, *are surveyed* on a rigidly accurate plan, at the expense of the government. This is the corner-stone of the system. In this consists its great improvement upon the land-system of Virginia, according to which warrants were granted to those entitled to receive them, for tracts of unsurveyed public land. These warrants might be *located* on any land not previously appropriated. In the absence of geometrical surveys, it was difficult, by natural boundaries, Indian paths, and buffalo traces, to identify the spots appropriated; the consequence was, that numerous warrants were laid on the same tract, conflicting claims arose, and the land titles of the country were brought into a state of the most perplexing and injurious embarrassment. The state of Kentucky, and that portion of Ohio, allotted as bounty-lands to the Virginia troops, have constituted one great theatre of litigation from their first settlement. On the other hand, land titles acquired under the system of the United States, are almost wholly exempt from controversies arising from uncertainty of location or boundary.

The surveys of the public lands of the United States are founded upon a series of true meridians. The first principal meridian is in Ohio, the second in Indiana, the third in Illinois, &c., each forming the base of a series of surveys, of which the lines are made to correspond, so that the whole country is at last divided into squares of one mile each, and townships of six miles each; and these subdivisions are distributed with mathematical accuracy into parallel ranges. The greatest division of land marked out by the survey is called a *township*, and contains 23,040 acres, being six English or American square miles. The township is subdivided into thirty-six equal portions or square miles, by lines crossing each other at right angles; these portions are called *sections*. The section contains 640 acres, and is subdivided into four parts, called *quarter sections*, each of which, of course, contains 160 acres. The quarter sections are finally divided into two parts, called *half quarter sections*, of eighty acres each, and this is the smallest regular subdivision known to the system. The sectional and quarter sectional divisions are designated by appropriate marks in the field, which are of a character to be easily distinguished from each other. The half quarter sections are not marked in the field, but are designated on the plan* or map of the survey, by the surveyor-general marking the distance on one of the ascertained lines, in order to get the quantity of such half quarter sections as exhibited by his plan of survey. The fractional sections, which contain less than 160 acres, are not subdivided: the fractional sections, which contain 160 acres and upwards, are subdivided in such manner as to preserve the most compact and convenient forms.

A series of contiguous townships, laid off from north to south, is called a *range*. The ranges are numbered north and south from the base or standing line running due east and west. They are counted from the standard meridian east and west.

The dividing lines of the sections, of course, run by the cardinal points, except where what is called a fractional section is created by a navigable river

* Termed "plot" in the American authority.

or an Indian boundary. The superintendence of the surveys is committed to five surveyors-general. One thirty-sixth part of all the land surveyed, being section number sixteen in each township, is reserved from sale for the support of schools in the township, and other reservations have been made for colleges and universities. All salt springs and lead mines are also reserved, and are subject to be leased under the direction of the President of the United States. Whenever the public interest is supposed to require that a certain portion of territory should be brought into market, for the accommodation of settlers or others who may wish to become purchasers, the president issues instructions to the surveyor-general, through the commissioner of the general land office at Washington, to have such portion of territory surveyed. The surveyor-general makes this requisition publicly known to those individuals who are in the habit of contracting for public surveys; and a contract for the execution of the surveys required is entered into between the surveyor-general and deputy surveyors. The contract is given to the lowest bidder, provided the surveyor-general be fully satisfied of his capacity to fulfil the contract. The *maximum* price established by law for executing the public surveys is three dollars a mile, in the upland and prairie countries. In the southern parts of the United States, where the surveys are rendered difficult by the occurrence of *bayous*, lakes, swamps, and cane-brakes, the maximum price established by law is four dollars a mile.

The deputy surveyors are bound by their contract to report to the surveyor-general the field-notes of the survey of each township, together with a plot of the township. From these field-notes the surveyor-general is enabled to try the accuracy of the plot returned by the deputy surveyor, and of the calculations of the quantity in the legal subdivisions of the tract surveyed. From these documents three plans or maps are caused to be prepared by the surveyor-general; one for his own office; one for the register of the proper land office, to guide him in the sale of the land; and the third for the commissioner of the general land office at Washington. The government has generally found it expedient to authorise the surveying of forty townships of land annually, in each land district, so as to admit of two sales by public auction annually, of twenty townships each.

The general land office at Washington is under the superintendence of an officer called commissioner of the general land office. It is subordinate to the treasury department.

The public lands are laid off into districts, in

each of which there is a land office, under the superintendence of two officers, appointed by the president and senate, called the register of the land office, and the receiver of public moneys. There are at present forty-two land officers. The register and the receiver each receive a salary of five hundred dollars *per annum*, and a commission of one per cent on the moneys paid into their office.

Till 1820 a credit was allowed on all purchases of public lands: in consequence of this system, large quantities of land had been purchased on speculation: and also in the ordinary course of purchases a vast amount of land-debt to the government had been contracted. To relieve the embarrassed condition of these debtors, an act was passed, authorizing the relinquishment of lands purchased, and substituting cash payments for the credit system. The most beneficial effects have resulted from this change, apart from the relief of those who were indebted to the government: at the same time the *minimum* price of the land was reduced from two dollars to one dollar and twenty-five cents an acre. In the first instance the public lands are offered for sale, under proclamations of the president, by public auction, with the limitation of the *minimum* rate. Lands not thus sold are afterwards subject to entry at private sale, and at the *minimum* price.

A very large amount of public land is in the occupation of persons who have settled upon it without title. This is frequently done in consequence of unavoidable delays in bringing the land into market, and not from any intention, on the part of the settler, to delay payment. Laws have been passed granting to settlers of this description a pre-emptive right in the acquisition of a title; that is, the preference over all other persons, in entering the land, at private sale. These laws afford the actual settler no protection against those who might choose to over-bid him at the public sales; but it is believed that in most cases, by mutual agreement among purchasers, the actual settler is enabled to obtain his land, even at public sale, at the *minimum* price. It is stated, however, that great injury is done to the settlers by combinations of land speculators, who infest the public sales, purchasing the lands at the minimum price, and compelling *bona fide* settlers to take them at an enhanced valuation. Should the settler refuse such an agreement, the speculators enter into competition with him at the sale. On the whole, it would appear that, on an average, the government obtains but the minimum price for its lands, although the quantity actually sold and occupied, being the choice of the whole quantity brought into market, is of course worth much more.

It has been suggested, and with an appearance of justice, that the price of the public lands is too high. The government, having already reimbursed itself for the cost of them, cannot be considered as having any other duty to perform than to promote their settlement as rapidly as it can take place by a healthy process, and to meet the wishes of all who desire *bona fide* to occupy them. Considering the class of men most likely to take the lead in settling a new country, one hundred dollars (the price of a half quarter-section) paid in cash to the government, is a tax too heavy, perhaps, for the privilege of taking up a farm in an unimproved wilderness. The price is already too low to oppose a serious obstacle to speculation: a considerable reduction of it would not, probably, increase that evil, while it would essentially relieve the *bona fide* settler. There would, in fact, perhaps, be little else to object to a plan of gratuitous donation of a half-quarter section to actual settlers, than the comparative injustice of such a plan towards those settlers who have already purchased their farms.

A novel and singular claim has been set up in some of the new states to the entire property of the public lands within their limits. The nature of this work does not require an examination of this claim; to enforce which no attempt has as yet been practically made.

It ought to be observed, that five per cent on all the sales of public lands within the states severally is reserved; three-fifths of which are to be expended by congress, in making roads leading to the states; and two-fifths to be expended by the states in the encouragement of learning. The first part of this reservation has been expended on the Cumberland road; and the treasury of the United States is greatly in advance to that fund, on account of this public work.

The total number of acres belonging to the United States is 1,062,463,171.

But the mode of disposing of the public lands, *if their sale for the profit of the government be dispensed with*, may give rise to much difficulty, in seeking to reconcile the interests of the United States with those of each of the states of the union. On this important point, Mr M'Lane, with his usual ability, thus observes:—

"It must be admitted that the public lands were ceded by the states, or subsequently acquired by the United States, for the common benefit; and that each state has an interest in their proceeds of which it cannot be justly deprived. Over this part of the public property the powers of the general government have been uniformly supposed to have a peculiarly extensive scope, and have been construed to authorise their application to purposes of education and improvement to which other branches of revenue were not deemed applicable. It is not practicable to keep the public lands out of the market; and the present mode of disposing of them is not believed to be the most profitable, either to the general government or to the states; and must be expected, when the proceeds shall be no longer required for the public debt, to give rise to new and more serious objections."

"Under these circumstances, it is submitted to the wisdom of congress to decide upon the propriety of disposing of all the public lands, in the aggregate, to those states, within whose territorial limits they lie, at a fair price, to be settled in such a manner as might be satisfactory to all. The aggregate price of the whole may then be apportioned among the several states of the union, according to such equitable ratio as may be consistent with the objects of the original cession; and the proportion of each may be paid or secured directly to the others by the respective states purchasing the land. All cause of difficulty with the general government, on this subject, would then be removed; and no doubt can be entertained, that, by means of stock issued by the buying states, bearing a moderate interest, and which, in consequence of the reimbursement of the public debt, would acquire a great value, they would be able at once to pay the amount upon advantageous terms. It may not be unreasonable also to expect, that the obligation to pay the annual interest upon the stock thus created, would diminish the motive for selling the lands at prices calculated to impair the greater value of that kind of property."

"It is believed, moreover, that the interests of the several states would be better promoted by such a disposition of the public domain, than by sales in the mode hitherto adopted; and it would, at once, place at the disposal of all the states of the union, upon fair terms, a fund for the purposes of education and improvement, of inestimable benefit to the future prosperity of the nation."—See Report on the Finances of the United States, of Dec. 1831.

The above details, principally from the American Almanac, are compiled from and collated with the Land Laws published by congress; Report from the Treasury to the Senate of the United States, February 1827; Report of a Select Committee of the House of Representatives of the United States, 1829; North American Review; American Quarterly; Seybert's Statistics, &c. &c.

## CHAPTER XVII.

Gold Mines.—Mint.

GOLD has hitherto, I believe, been discovered only in North Carolina, South Carolina, Virginia and Georgia, at least in any quantity.

The first notice of gold, from North Carolina, on the records of the mint, occurs in the year 1814, during which it was received to the amount of 11,000 dollars. It continued to be received during the succeeding years, until 1824 inclusive, in different quantities, but all inferior to that of 1814, and on an average not exceeding 2500 dollars a year. In 1825, the amount received was 17,000 dollars; in 1826, 20,000 dollars; in 1827, about 21,000 dollars; in 1828, nearly 46,000 dollars; and in 1829, 128,000 dollars.*

In 1825, there was published in the "American Journal of Science and the Arts," an account of these mines by Professor Olmsted, who estimated the gold country at only 1000 square miles; but it has since been found to be vastly more extensive;

* Vide American Journal of Science and the Arts.

and a succession of gold mines has been discovered in the country lying to the east of the Blue Ridge, extending from the vicinity of the river Potomac into the State of Alabama. These mines are now wrought, to a greater or less extent, in the states of Virginia, North Carolina, South Carolina and Georgia.

In an account of a Tour in North Carolina, published in a New York Journal, there is mention made of the gold mines. From this writer we learn that the state is rich in gold mines. The gold is far more extensive in that state than is generally supposed; it commences in Virginia, and extends south-west through North Carolina, nearly in the middle of the state as regards its length; along the northern part of South Carolina into Georgia, and thence north-westwardly into Alabama, and ends in Tennessee. The mines in North Carolina and Georgia are now worked to a great extent; those of Virginia and South Carolina to a small extent; and those in Tennessee have not been worked at all, although it is probable that they will be soon. In this state, the counties of Burke and Rutherford contains the best *gold washings*, as they are called; that is, the gold there is found in small and *pure* particles mixed with the sand, which lies in deposits, as if it occupied (as the miners believe) the beds of what were once streams of water, creeks, rivers, &c. The gold is there obtained by washing away the sand, and it is a simple process. But the counties of Mecklenburg, Rowan, Davidson and Cabarras, are the richest in what may be properly called gold *mines;* that is, where the gold is found in *ore*, and not distinguishable by the eye, and which is separated by smelting, using quicksilver for the purpose of detaching the gold from the gross earthy substances. This is done by first pounding the ore (what the miners call stamping it), then grinding it, mixed with the quicksilver, to a fine powder (like flour), and afterwards distilling the whole in an alembic, which separates the quicksilver from the gold. This part of the business is simple and easy; but to become an expert and skilful *miner*, to detect gold in the ore with certainty, and to know how to conduct, if I may say so, the perforations, that is, sinking shafts (like wells), and forming and fortifying galleries or horizontal perforations to reach the veins, &c. requires great ingenuity as well as experience.

The best veins of gold are not horizontal, nor often vertical, but have a dip of forty-five degrees to the horizon. They vary in width from a few inches to several feet. They are not confined to hills at all, but are found also in the low lands. These veins are often parallel to each other at unequal distances. Their depth in most places has not been ascertained. There have been no shafts sunk lower than one hundred and twenty feet. In some of the mines the galleries, or lateral perforations (or arched entries, as they may be called), extend a great distance in various directions from the main shafts, and so reach the veins. They are usually about twenty feet, one above another, which enables the miners to work with the greatest advantage.

These mines have not been worked to any considerable extent for more than about five or six years, or probably much less. And yet many of them are worked upon an extensive scale, and mills for grinding the ore, propelled by water or by steam, are erected in vast numbers. The company of Messrs Bissels, which is one of the most considerable, employs about 600 hands. The whole number of men now employed at the mines in these southern states is at least 20,000. The weekly value of these mines is estimated at 100,000 dollars, or more than one million sterling annually. But a small part of the gold is sent to the United States' mint. By far the larger part is sent to Europe, particularly to Paris.

Of the working miners the greater number are

foreigners—Germans, Swiss, Swedes, Spaniards, English, Welsh, Scotch, &c. There are no less than *thirteen* different languages spoken at the mines in this state! And men are flocking to the mines from all parts, and find ready employment. Hundreds of land-owners and renters work the mines on their grounds on a small scale, not being able to encounter the expense of much machinery. The state of morals among the miners or labourers is represented to be deplorably bad. This may be attributed to the absence of any general organization as yet for the police and regulation of the mines, combined with the usual effects of gold upon the uneducated and needy classes of men (often not the most favourable specimens of their various nations), who generally seek employment in the gold districts. The village of Charlotte, in Mecklenburg county, is in the immediate vicinity of several of the largest mines. It is increasing rapidly.

One interesting fact deserves mention:—when speaking of the gold mines, there are indubitable evidences that these mines were known and *worked* by the aboriginal inhabitants, or some other people, at a remote period. Many pieces of machinery which were used for this purpose have been found. Among them are several *crucibles* of earthenware, and far better than those now in use. Messrs Bissels have tried three of them, and found that they lasted twice or three times as long as even the Hessian crucibles, which are the best now made. It is to be regretted that some antiquarian has not had an opportunity of at least examining these curious relics; and it is hoped that they will be preserved in future, notwithstanding the temptation offered by their superior qualities.

These gold mines prove that the whole region in which they abound was once under the powerful action of fire. And it is a fact, not generally known, that the miners who have come from the mines in South America and in Europe, pronounce this region to be more abundant in gold than any other that has been found on the globe. There is no telling the extent of these mines: but sufficient is known to prove they are of vast extent.

It is not easy to ascertain the number of mines which are now opened; it is, however, very great, and constantly increasing. These mining establishments are of every variety as to extent of operations.

There is a vast amount of capital invested by the different companies which are now embarked in this business. A large portion of this capital belongs to foreigners.

Since the year 1827, the gold mines of Virginia

have also attracted considerable attention. The belt of country in which they are found extends through Spotsylvania and some neighbouring counties. The gold region abounds in quartz, which contains cubes of sulphuret of iron. These cubes are often partly or totally decomposed, and the cells thus created are sometimes filled with gold. The gold is found on the surface, and in the structure of quartz; but in greatest abundance resting upon slate, and in its fissures. The gold is diffused over large surfaces, and has not yet been found sufficiently in mass, except in a few places, to make mining profitable. The method of obtaining the metal is by filtration, or washing the earth, and by an amalgam of quicksilver. The average value of the earth yielding gold is stated at twenty cents a bushel.

In the annual report for 1829, the progressive development of the gold region of the United States was illustrated by referring to the increase of the annual receipts from North Carolina, which, previous to 1824, had been inconsiderable, but from that year to 1829, inclusive, had advanced from 5000 dollars to 128,000 dollars; and also to the then novel occurrence of gold having been received at the mint from Virginia and South Carolina, about 2500 dollars having been received from the former and 3500 dollars from the latter. The year 1830 exhibits, in relation to all these states, a conspicuous increase in the production of gold, and presents also the remarkable fact of 212,000 dollars in gold received from Georgia, from which state no specimen thereof had been received at the mint in any previous year.

The following statement, taken from the report of the director of the mint, January 1, 1831, will show the amount of gold received from the different states, as well as that from other countries, in the course of the year 1830.

The coinage, during the year 1830, amounted to

| | Dollars. |
|---|---|
| Gold coins . . | 643,105 |
| Silver ditto . . | 2,495,400 |
| Copper . . . | 17,115 |
| Total . | 3,155,620 |

The description of coins was as follows:

| | | | Dollars. |
|---|---|---|---|
| Half eagles . . | 126,351 | making | 631,755 |
| Quarter eagles . . | 4,540 | . | 11,350 |
| Half dollars . . | 4,764,800 | . | 2,382 400 |
| Dimes . . . | 510,000 | . | 51,000 |
| Half dimes . . | 1,240,000 | . | 62,000 |
| Cents . . . | 1,711,500 | . | 17,115 |
| Total number of pieces . | 8,357,191 | Total | 3,155,620 |

Of the gold coined in the course of 1830, there was imported from

| | Dollars. |
|---|---|
| Mexico, South America, West Indies, about . . | 125,000 |
| Africa . . . | 19,000 |
| United States . . | 466,000 |
| Sources not ascertained . | 33,000 |
| Total . | 643,000 |

Of the gold found in the United States, amounting in value to about 100,000*l.* sterling, mentioned in the foregoing statement, there came from

| | Dollars. |
|---|---|
| Georgia, about . . | 212,000 |
| North Carolina . . | 204,000 |
| South Carolina . . | 26,000 |
| Virginia . . . | 24,000 |
| Total produce in the United States | 466,000 |

## CHAPTER XVIII.

Cultivation ot sugar in Louisiana.—Florida.—Slavery.

THE whole produce of sugar in Louisiana, in the year 1828, has been stated at 88,878 hogsheads of 1000 pounds each. The number of sugar estates above 700, and the capital invested in them about forty-five millions of dollars; but every year the increasing investments, and more than proportionate increase in the quantity of sugar made, renders this estimate but of little use at the present moment.

In Florida, also, the cultivation of sugar has made great progress. I am indebted to the kindness of M. Achille Murat* for the following details on the sugar cultivation of Florida; but I have no means at present of ascertaining the amount of capital now invested in the cultivation of the cane of that state.

It would appear quite certain that in Florida, with a very moderate capital and some prudence and activity, a very large return is to be obtained for money invested in sugar plantations; and, with

* M. Achille Murat, it may be recollected, left Europe some years ago, and purchased land in Florida. He has become an adopted citizen of the United States, where his merit and abilities are duly appreciated.

perseverance, a large fortune may be realized with comparative certainty. The cultivation of sugar in that state is as yet in its infancy; but a European can with difficulty imagine the rapidity with which improvements take place in the United States generally; and where the cultivation of the south succeeds, the profits are still more encouraging than in the slower returns of northern industry. A few years ago the greater part of Florida was almost a wilderness; now Tallahassee is a flourishing town, and great part of the state owes its growing prosperity, as I am informed, to the cultivation of sugar.

According to Colonel Murat's computation, a purchase of 240 acres may be made at three dollars an acre; and a plantation stocked with all the necessary tools, provisions, mules, ploughs, clothing for the negroes, &c. for little more than £1000. In this sum is included the value of ten slaves; for the curse of slavery attends the cultivation of sugar in the United States, as elsewhere. Let us hope that it may be practicable at a future time to continue it without this blot upon the growing fortunes of America, although M. Murat certainly holds out little prospect of such a consummation.

With this moderate outlay, and no material addition to it for the space of three or four years, a return of nearly 100 per cent may be obtained.

Indeed, land may be purchased at half the sum mentioned above, if at a distance from towns, &c.; and, by a judicious alternation of other crops, as cotton, maize, &c. very little risk or expense need be incurred by the cultivator.

The Americans have frequently been reproached for suffering the continuance of slavery for one instant after the declaration of independence. It must be recollected that before that time they were not allowed to abolish it, even after repeated petitions to that effect to the government of the mother country.

But any person who has an opportunity of observing personally the effects of the existence of this dreadful evil must, I think, allow that a sudden and unprepared emancipation would probably be productive, in the first instance at least, of evils a thousand-fold greater to all the parties concerned than even its unmitigated continuance. It is not one of the least lamentable effects of slavery, that it is apt to unfit both the oppressor* and the victim

* I use not these terms invidiously; Captain Hall, M. Vigne, and many succeeding travellers, bear witness to the general kindness with which the slaves are treated in the United States. But it is a *system*, wherever it exists, whose whole existence rests upon a foundation of injustice, outrage, and the most atrocious robbery, that of the liberty, I may say the life (or its usufruct) of a fellow-creature. This right of an unoffending individual to his liberty may be disputed by those who argue with Dumont as

for a different state of things; and as a question of interest, it may be regarded as an alternative of wealth and power, or complete ruin to the slave-

to the inherent rights of our nature, and would make them depend upon a legal title. " La declaration des droits peut se faire *après la constitution*, mais non pas avant, *car les droits existent par les lois*, et ne les precedent pas," &c. Legislators, he asserts, must not be tied by general maxims false in themselves. *Les hommes naissent libres et égaux*, cela n'est pas vrai. Ils ne naissent point libres, au contraire, ils naissent dans un état de faiblesse et de dépendance nécessaire; *égaux*—où le sont ils? où pourront ils l'être? entend-t'on l'égalité de fortune, de talent, de vertu, d'industrie, de condition? le mensonge est manifeste. Il faut des volumes pour parvenir à donner un certain sens raisonnable à cette égalité, que vous proclamez sans exception," &c. &c.—*Vide Dumont's Mirabeau, French edition*, p. 98.

By an extension of this principle there are no moral or personal rights co-existent with our being, and drawing their origin from the same inscrutable source that gives us life; but they depend entirely on the law of the land. This is an excellent argument for lawyers, as, carried to the farthest limit, it would declare that in every country, whatever may be the nature of the law, if it order the destruction of prisoners, or their conversion into roast meat, or the mastication, by instalments, of living offenders against the rights of a husband, as in Sumatra; in short, whatever the law decrees becomes alone an inherent right.

To confine ourselves, however, to civilized nations, the United States cut the knot at once, by beginning their declaration with a formula, that legally gives this right, if not already in existence, and slavery is a continual infraction of it, not legalized by the federal union, but by the enactments of particular states.

Finally, no theory has been more misunderstood than that of the liberty and equality of men *subject to the law*, in America. No constitution can render the fortunes, conditions, or abilities of men equal, any more than it can make any two persons physically or morally precisely similar; or two leaves of the same tree perfectly alike; nor was such an interpretation, I should holders in many cases. Can we be surprised at the obstacles that are opposed to any general abolition of this (almost universally) allowed evil, by those states of America whose culture and existence seem at present to depend on it? Let us turn from what must unfortunately be regarded for the present as a necessary evil, admitting of no *immediate* remedy that human prudence can adopt, to consider the admirable and practicable mode in which the existence of slavery has been done away with in the northern, eastern, and other considerable states in the union—in a word, in its most

think, ever seriously intended. The natural differences of talent, person, disposition, &c. produce the corresponding distinctions among men, which *artificial* distinction becomes their right, by the same principle that secured the fruition of their natural advantages. Certain other artificial rights, however, depending upon the accidents of birth, and having force of law in other countries, are, by the principles dominant in the United States, abolished. The natural dependence of man in infancy on the protection of his parents is by no means disturbed by the theory of political independence. This helplessness causes the contraction of a debt of reciprocity of the good offices that the child receives from its parents, to be at a future period repaid when the infant itself becomes a parent. The rights to charitable protection and support possessed by the infirm in mind or body, depend upon a similar implied mutuality of good offices, whenever the want of them may be felt by those by whom they are now conferred. Revealed, or even what is called natural religion, shows that these common rights of mankind necessarily exist, at least in civilized communities, whether before or after the creation of a legal claim.

rapidly improving sections. By enacting the prospective emancipation of certain slaves at fixed periods, and the birthright of liberty to those born after certain tèrms, slavery has disappeared in states where it formerly extensively existed: and this extinction of so foul a stain has taken place without danger or difficulty, by the present mode of carrying it into execution. It may be in my power at a future time to offer some observations on subjects connected with the extinction of slavery, which the limits and nature of this work preclude.

A serious obstacle to the advantageous emancipation of negroes in the United States, is the extraordinary prejudice of colour. Europeans can hardly conceive the force with which this absurd and unjust prejudice acts in America, not only against those whose blood is unmixed, but against those coloured persons whom it requires much experience, and perhaps legal evidence to discover, as being under the ban of this exclusive aristocracy of complexion. If an individual, concentrating the wisdom and virtues of every age in his own person, and inheriting the qualities of a Socrates, an Alfred, a Gustavus Vasa, and a Washington combined, were born with a *negro* skin in the United States, I do not think that he would ever be allowed *a perfectly social equality with a white scoundrel.* The consequence of this artificial and unjust social degradation is not unfrequently a real debasement, which often renders the free coloured population comparatively unprofitable members of society.

Those who have the interests of their country at heart, and look with a prophetic eye, not only to the interests of humanity, but to those of policy, have long wished to do away with so great a source of weakness and unhappiness as the existence of slavery in the United States, and at the same time to secure for those emancipated a home, where the practice of the principles laid down by the declaration of independence will not be at variance with its theory. With this view the establishment of a colony was proposed so early as the year 1796, by a distinguished Friend or Quaker, named Gerard Hopkins; but it did not produce much useful effect until General C. F. Mercer, the Wilberforce of the American Congress, opened a correspondence with the philanthropists of the different states, which led to the formation of the American Colonization Society, in 1817.

"The great objects of that society, were—the final and entire abolition of slavery, providing for the best interests of the blacks, by establishing them in independence upon the coast of Africa; thus constituting them the protectors of the unfortunate natives against the inhuman ravages of the slaver, and seeking, through them, to spread the lights of civilization and Christianity among the *fifty millions* who inhabit those dark regions. To meet the views of all parties, they had a most difficult path to tread; but as all legislation on the subject of slavery was *specially reserved to the respective states by the Articles of Confederation, and had become the basis of the Constitution of the United States*, they very wisely, instead of denouncing an evil which they had not the power to overthrow, had recourse to the more sure, but gradual mode of removing it, by enlightening the consciences, and convincing the judgments, of the slave-holders. Their theory is justified by experience; for while our little colony has grown quite as fast as could be wished for by its most judicious friends, these principles have been silently gaining ground in the slave states, yet so rapidly, *that the number of slaves offered gratuitously by benevolent owners, exceed ten-fold the present means of the society to receive and convey them to Africa.* The disposition of Virginia has been already shown. Delaware and Kentucky have also proved their anxiety to concur in so noble a cause; and Dr Ayres, the earliest governor of Liberia, now resident at Maryland, asserts, 'that owing to the plans and principles of colonization being better understood, in less than twenty years there will be no more slaves born in that state.'

"A party in South Carolina is now almost the only opponent that the society has at home; and, as if to afford the most incontestable evidence that its plan will destroy the institution of slavery in the United States, they ground their opposition upon the *inevitable tendency* of colonization *to eradicate slave-holding*, and thereby deprive them of their *property*.

"But if the present means of the society are inadequate to effect its purposes, it will be recollected that only eight years have elapsed since Cape Messurado, then a mart for the sale of 10,000 fellow-creatures annually, was purchased from the natives; that unhallowed traffic has been entirely destroyed; a flourishing colony of 2000 emancipated slaves has been founded; churches, schools, commerce, and even a newspaper established, and the confidence of the aborigines so completely won, that 10,000 of them are, as allies of this new republic, participating in the blessings of civilization and religion.

"The feelings of these happy people are best

described in their circular to the people of colour of the United States. Knowing that in the infancy of the society some had impugned its motives, and others doubted its success, they pointedly observe —'*judge, then, of the feelings with which we hear the motives and doings of the Colonization Society traduced—and that, too, by men too ignorant to know what the society had accomplished—too weak to look through its plans and intentions—or too dishonest to acknowledge either.*' All their letters unite in grateful thanks for the great blessings conferred upon them; and even greater are either realizing, or in prospect, for the savage tribes around. All this has been effected for the small sum of 27,000*l.*; and its friends, at first but few, have so increased, in number and confidence, that one third of their total receipts accrued during the last year; several religious bodies have given it their earnest and unanimous support; thirteen of the states have recommended it to the patronage of congress; and* on the elevation of its champion, the Hon. Henry Clay, to the presidency, there cannot be a doubt that funds adequate to the fulfilment of this glorious design will be granted by the general government.

* It must be recollected that these are the words and sentiments of the editor of the Report of the Colonization Society.

"If the very dregs of the human race (the slavers) can drag annually from Africa 100,000 unfortunate wretches, will it be doubted that the energies of a free people can restore half as many of her descendants, when prompted alike by duty and interest?—this, in a few years, would effect a cure of the evil?—the sum required is too small to be an obstacle. It has been shown in parliament that during the last twenty-four years about 8,000,000*l*. has been spent upon Sierra Leone. That sum, divided into thirty instalments, would, in as many years, settle our whole coloured population in the land of their ancestors. Nor can it fail to give the society increased confidence in the soundness of their own system, when they find that ministers have announced their intention of regulating the African colonies of England upon the same plan, and elevating the black man, by conferring upon his race the principal offices of the different posts. Neither has our scheme been unsanctioned by the approval of some of the best men of Britain—Richard Dykes Alexander, a name ever prominent in deeds of practical philanthropy, 'convinced that a more rapid progress was never known in any colony towards comfort and respectability than that of Liberia, published an appeal in its behalf; in consequence of which, the following sums were sent to Barnetts, Hoare and Co., 62 Lombard-street, who continue to act as bankers to the fund, viz." (here follows a list of subscribers to assist this praiseworthy undertaking). "Each *7l.* 10*s.* of which not only secures the freedom of a slave and pays his passage to Africa, but constitutes him a freeholder of thirty acres of fertile land.

"Hence, the undersigned, as representative of the AMERICAN COLONIZATION SOCIETY, feels himself justified in drawing the same conclusion, which, he believes, the wise and good of all sects and all parties in the United States have arrived at—that it is the happy means, destined by a kind providence, for securing to Africa the fulfilment of the glorious promises in her behalf—by effecting, in the mode most consistent with their interest and happiness, the freedom of her coloured population —*et pari passu*, destroying that inhuman traffic which has so long been the affliction of Africa, the disgrace of Europe, and the sourge of America.

"ELLIOTT CRESSON."

It is unnecessary for me to add any thing to the above extract to show the views and principles of this excellent and practical undertaking, which at a comparatively small expense has effected so much without the assistance of any government, or much loss from the effects of a climate, to which the coloured population become soon habituated.

Some idea of the happy effects already resulting from this undertaking, may be formed from such quotations as this, taken by chance from an American paper.

"There arrived at the American colony in Africa, from the 9th to the 29th of January, one ship, seven brigs, and three schooners, besides vessels belonging to the colonists; among them were a brig from France, a ship from Liverpool, and three brigs and a schooner from the United States. Some of the colonists are said to be worth from 10 to 15,000 dollars."—*Nat. Gazette, April* 1831.

The report* of the American Colonization Society affords ample evidence of the present utility and good prospects of the colony†. It contains

* The Reports of the Pennsylvania Colonization Society are to be found at Miller's and other booksellers in London.

† "The true character of the African climate is not well understood in other countries. Its inhabitants are as robust, as healthy, as long-lived, to say the least, as those of any other country. Nothing like an epidemic has ever appeared in this colony; nor can we learn from the natives, that the calamity of a sweeping sickness ever yet visited this part of the continent. But the change from a temperate to a tropical country is a great one—too great not to affect the health, more or less—and, in the case of old people, and very young children, it often causes death. In the early years of the colony, want of good houses, the great fatigues and dangers of the settlers, their irregular mode of living, and the hardships and discouragements they met with, greatly helped the other causes of sickness, which prevailed to an alarm-

**also a speech of Mr Clay's on this subject, highly worthy of perusal.**

ing extent, and were attended with great mortality. But we look back to those times as to a season of trial long past,and nearly forgotten. Our houses and circumstances are now comfortable; and, for the last two or three years, not one person in forty, from the Middle and Southern States, has died from the change of climate. The disastrous fate of the company of settlers who came out from Boston in the brig Vine, eighteen months ago, is an exception to the common lot of emigrants, and the causes of it ought to be explained. Those people left a cold region in the coldest part of winter, and arrived here in the hottest season of our year. Many of them were too old to have survived long in any country. They most imprudently neglected the prescriptions of our very successful physician, the Rev. Lot Carey, who has great experience and great skill in the fevers of the country, and depended on medicines brought with them, which could not fail to prove injurious. And, in consequence of all these unfortunate circumstances, their sufferings were severe, and many died. But we are not apprehensive that a similar calamity will befall any future emigrants, except under similar disadvantages.

"People now arriving have comfortable houses to receive them; will enjoy the regular attendance of a physician in the slight sickness that may await them; will be surrounded and attended by healthy and happy people, who have borne the effects of the climate, and who will encourage and fortify them against that despondency which, alone, has carried off several in the first years of the colony.

"But you may say, that even health and freedom, as good as they are, are still dearly paid for, when they cost you the common comforts of life, and expose your wives and children to famine, and all the evils of want and poverty. We do not dispute the soundness of this conclusion either; but we utterly deny that it has any application to the people of Liberia.

"Away with all the false notions that are circulating about the barrenness of this country: they are the observations of such ignorant or designing men as would injure both it and you. A

The penitentiary system of the United States is well deserving of attention. Although the peniten-

more fertile soil, and a more productive country, so far as it is cultivated, there is not, we believe, on the face of the earth. Its hills and its plains are covered with a verdure which never fades; the productions of nature keep on in their growth through all the seasons of the year. Even the natives of the country, almost without farming tools, without skill, and with very little labour, make more grain and vegetables than they can consume, and often more than they can sell.

"Cattle, swine, fowls, ducks, goats and sheep, thrive without feeding, and require no other care than to keep them from straying. Cotton, coffee, indigo, and the sugar-cane, are all the spontaneous growth of our forests; and may be cultivated, at pleasure, to any extent, by such as are disposed. The same may be said of rice, Indian-corn, Guinea-corn, millet, and too many species of fruits and vegetables to be enumerated. Add to all this, we have no dreary winter here, for one half of the year to consume the productions of the other half. Nature is constantly renewing herself, and constantly pouring her treasures, all the year round, into the laps of the industrious. We could say on this subject more; but we are afraid of exciting, too highly, the hopes of the imprudent. It is only the industrious and virtuous that we can point to independence, and plenty, and happiness, in this country. Such people are nearly sure to attain, in a very few years, to a style of comfortable living, which they may in vain hope for in the United States; and, however short we come of this character ourselves, it is only a due acknowledgement of the bounty of Divine Providence to say, that we generally enjoy the good things of this life to our entire satisfaction.

"Our trade is chiefly confined to the coast, to the interior parts of the continent, and to foreign vessels. It is already valuable, and fast increasing. It is carried on in the productions of the country, consisting of rice, palm oil, ivory, tortoise-shell, dyewoods, gold, hides, wax, and a small amount of coffee; and it brings us, in return, the products and manufactures of the four quarters of the world. Seldom, indeed, is our harbour clear of tiaries generally can hardly be classed among sources of revenue, yet in more than one instance in America

European and American shipping; and the bustle and thronging of our streets show something, already, of the activity of the smaller sea-ports of the United States.

"Mechanics, of nearly every trade, are carrying on their various occupations; their wages are high; and a large number would be sure of constant and profitable employment.

"Not a child or youth in the colony but is provided with an appropriate school. We have a numerous public library, and a court-house, meeting-houses, school-houses, and fortifications sufficient, or nearly so, for the colony in its present state.

"Our houses are constructed of the same materials, and finished in the same style as in the towns of America. We have abundance of good building stone, shells for lime, and clay, of an excellent quality, for bricks. Timber is plentiful, of various kinds, and fit for all the different purposes of building and fencing.

"Truly, we have a goodly heritage; and if there is any thing lacking in the character or condition of the people of this colony, it never can be charged to the account of the country: it must be the fruit of our own mismanagement, or slothfulness, or vices. But from these evils we confide in Him, to whom we are indebted for all our blessings, to preserve us. It is the topic of our weekly and daily thanksgiving to Almighty God, both in public and in private, and He knows with what sincerity that we were ever conducted, by his Providence, to this shore. Such great favours, in so short a time, and mixed with so few trials, are to be ascribed to nothing but his special blessing. This we acknowledge. We only want the gratitude which such signal favours call for. Nor are we willing to close this paper without adding a heartfelt testimonial of the deep obligations we owe to our American patrons and best earthly benefactors, whose wisdom pointed us to this home of our nation, and whose active and persevering benevolence enabled us to reach it. *Judge, then, of the feelings with which we hear the motives and doings of the Colonization Society traduced—and that, too, by men too ignorant to* they have been found not only to defray all the expenses of their establishment, but to leave a considerable balance of profit (derived from the labour of the prisoners), at the disposal of the state. There must consequently be some essential difference in the principles upon which these establishments are carried on in our own country, or we should not see grants of 20,000*l.* and upwards made towards the support of similar institutions, instead of a return produced by the prisoners, as it is not for want of convicts able to work that they continue so expensive in England.

*know what that society has accomplished; too weak to look through its plans and intentions; or too dishonest to acknowledge either.* But without pretending to any prophetic sagacity, we can certainly predict to that society, the ultimate triumph of their hopes and labours, and disappointment and defeat to all who oppose them. Men may theorize, and speculate about their plans in America, but there can be no speculation here. The cheerful abodes of civilization and happiness which are scattered over this verdant mountain—the flourishing settlements which are spreading around it—the sound of Christian instruction, and scenes of Christian worship, which are heard and seen in this land of brooding pagan darkness—a thousand contented freemen united in founding a new Christian empire, happy themselves, and the instruments of happiness to others—every object, every individual, is an argument, is demonstration, of the wisdom and goodness of the plan of colonization.

"*Where is the argument that shall refute facts like these? And where is the man hardy enough to deny them?*"—See Report of American Colonization Society, extract of a letter from a colonist, verbatim.

# SUMMARY.

Each individual pays annually towards the public expenditure as follows:

ACCORDING TO REVUE BRITANNIQUE, NO. 12, 1831.

| | | | *l.* | *s.* | *d.* |
|---|---|---|---|---|---|
| In France . | 31 francs . | or | 1 | 5 | 10 |
| In United States . | 35 francs . | or | 1 | 9 | 2 |

MR FENIMORE COOPER'S ESTIMATE.

In France gives no estimate.

In United States, i. e. a citizen of New York to the general and state governments, including principal and interest of public debt, schools, support of clergy, poor, internal improvements, &c. 14 francs 5 centimes or 0 11 $8\frac{}{2}$

Without the ecclesiastical expenses, the poor, or sums paid towards the extinction of the public debt, and interest upon it . 5 fr. 35 c. . or 0 4 $5\frac{1}{2}$

To the state of New York 95 c. . or 0 0 $9\frac{1}{2}$

GENERAL BERNARD'S CALCULATION.

In France, without clergy (and some other expenses before specified) . 28 fr. 12 c. . or 1 3 $5\frac{1}{10}$

| | | | | | |
|---|---|---|---|---|---|
| In United States, ditto | 11 fr. 47 c. . | or | 0 | 9 | $6\frac{6}{10}$ |
| In France, without the debt, | 20 fr. 57 c. . | or | 0 | 17 | $1\frac{6}{10}$ |
| In United States, ditto | 6 fr. 6 c. . | or | 0 | 5 | $0\frac{3}{10}$ |

In United States, maximum paid by each individual to state government . 1 fr. 32 . or 0 1 $1\frac{1}{10}$

Or to federal and state governments (exclusive of clergy) . . . . . . 0 10 $7\frac{7}{10}$

CAPTAIN BASIL HALL.

| | | | |
|---|---|---|---|
| In United States, to federal government . | 0 | 9 | $4\frac{3}{4}$ |
| Ditto state government . . . . . | 0 | 3 | 0 |
| Total . | 0 | 12 | $4\frac{3}{4}$ |

It would be superfluous to offer any detailed estimate after the above statements, particularly as the foregoing chapters and the tables in the Appendix will enable any person to make a calculation of the amount paid by each individual in the United States towards the public expenditure. It would appear, however, that the estimate of Mr Cooper is somewhat low. By adding the estimated amount paid to the clergy in the United States to General Bernard's estimate, we obtain with sufficient accuracy the real amount.

Allowing largely for the clergy, the state judiciaries, &c. and other items omitted by Captain Hall, added to the federal expenditure, the maximum annual amount may be about thirteen shillings.

| | *l.* | *s.* | *d.* |
|---|---|---|---|
| For the average expenditure of the United Kingdom during the years 1828–9 and 30, including the national debt, the clergy (of every denomination), and the poor-rates, an inhabitant of Great Britain pays a minimum of about . . . . . | 2 | 13 | 4 |
| Or, deducting the interest of national debt, say 28,000,000*l.* about . . . . . | 1 | 10 | 0 |
| Captain Hall, gives as mean amount paid by each individual in the United States, 12*s.* 4¾*d.* not including clergy, poor, &c. but excluding slaves, or persons not taxed . . . . . . | 0 | 14 | 5½ |

If we take from the calculation of the sum paid by each individual in the United Kingdom, the number of those supported by poor-rates, &c. it would at least balance the difference.

The expense of collecting the revenue in the United States, including what General Bernard calls *administration centrale*, is

| | |
|---|---|
| In United States . . . | 5 and $\frac{3}{10}$ per cent. |
| In France . . . . | 12 and $\frac{7}{10}$ per cent. |
| In England, according to Sir H. Parnell | 7 and $\frac{1}{2}$ per cent. |

But it is probable that Sir Henry Parnell only includes the expense, technically called "collection of the revenue" (lately, however, diminished in amount), and not the whole expense incurred by the maintenance of public offices, salaries, &c. of each department. The author of a pamphlet on "British Relations with the Chinese Empire," makes the expense of collection on 97,067,847*l.* to be in the years 1828-9 and 1830, 9,402,801*l.* or about ten per cent on the amount of import duties, spirits, malt-liquors, wine, sugar, coffee, tobacco, and stamps. Vide also Quarterly, 1825.

| | Dollars. | c. |
|---|---|---|
| The total expenditure of the federal government for 1831 is estimated at . . | 30,967,201 | 25 |
| including, however . . . | 16,189,289 | 00 |
| for the payments on the public debt. | | |
| Leaving as the amount for current expenditure, | 14,777,912 | 00 |
| or about £3,283,980. | | |

| | | |
|---|---|---|
| The receipts for 1832 are estimated at . | 30,100,000 | 00 |

| | | | |
|---|---|---|---|
| Viz. Customs | . | . | 26,500,000 |
| Public lands | . | . | 3,000,000 |
| Bank dividends | | . | 490,000 |
| Incidental receipts | | . | 110,000 |

| | Dollars. | c. |
|---|---|---|
| The total expenditure for 1832, exclusive of public debt . . . . | 13,365,202 | 16 |
| or about £2,970,045. | | |
| Leaving a balance of . . | 16,734,797 | 84 |

or about £3,718,843.—Vide Mr M'Lane's Report on the Finances of the United States.

# APPENDIX

*Extract from "Review of Captain B. Hall's Travels."*

"WITH regard to the judicial establishments of the two countries, he is perpetually referring, in the language of taunt, to the superior firmness of the tenure of office in England. It is plain, from every word he utters, that he is under a complete delusion as to the real state of the fact. In England the judges can be removed by a bare majority of the legislature, without any form of trial, or even an allegation of their having committed any offence. Paley states this with his usual correctness (*Principles of Moral and Political Philosophy*): 'As protection against every illegal attack upon the rights of the subject by the servants of the crown is to be sought for from these tribunals, the judges of the land become not unfrequently the arbitrators between the king and the people, on which account they ought to be independent of either; or what is the same thing, equally dependent on both; that is, if they be appointed by the one, they should be removable only by the other. This was the policy which dictated that memorable *improvement in our Constitution*, by which the judges, who, before the revolution, held their offices *during the pleasure of the king*, can now be *deprived* of them *only* by an address from both houses of parliament, as the most regular, solemn and authentic way by which the *dissatisfaction of the people* can be expressed.' Mr Hallam, in his Constitutional History (vol. i. p. 245), remarks, 'No judge can be dismissed from office except in consequence of a conviction for some offence, *or* the address of both houses of parliament, which is *tantamount to an act of legislature*." And thus the matter rests at the present day. The same casting vote which suffices to pass a law may dismiss the judge whose interpretation of it is not acceptable. This is not the case in any part of the United States. The judges of the national courts cannot be reached by address at all; they may defy the president and both houses of congress. In the states where this English provision has been copied, it has been rendered comparatively harmless by requiring the concurrence of *two-thirds* of each branch of the legislature in order to effect the removal.

"Let us suppose, for the sake of illustration, a question to arise on the emancipation bill, as it is called, of last session. The most strenuous supporters of that bill admitted it to be a violation of what they designated as the constitution of 1688. In Mr Peel's speech, less than a year before, he declared, 'If the constitution was to be considered the king, lords, and commons, it would be *subverting that constitution to* admit Roman Catholics to the privileges they sought; it would be an important change in the state of the *Constitution as established at the revolution*.' (*Speech in May* 1828.) Lord Tenderden, the chief justice of the court of king's bench, in resisting in the house of lords the bill subsequently introduced by Mr Peel himself, declared that 'he looked upon the proposed measure as leading by a broad and direct road to the overthrow of the Protestant Church.' (*Times, April* 6, 1829.) Suppose the sergeant-at-arms should thrust back Mr O'Connell on his attempting to enter the house of commons, or any other cause arise bringing up the act: were Lord Tenderden, as a judge, to use any language of an unsatisfactory kind, he might be hurled from his seat by that very legislature, which was induced to pass the law. In the United States the people have denied themselves this power. Mr Chief Justice Marshall might move intrepidly on, where Lord Chief Justice Tenderden must yield or be sacrificed. Congress *fairly* and *equally* represents the whole country, yet it has not the power of a British parliament to bring to bear on judges what Paley calls 'the displeasure of the people.'

"It is a subject of curious reflection, that until the constitution of 1688, or rather until the 13th year of Will. III., judges were, as Paley remarks, the creatures of the crown. The actual power of judicial appointment at present resides in Mr Peel, the home secretary. He has said that the constitution of 1688 would be subverted by measures which he has since urged through parliament; if so, the king has an unlimited power of making and unmaking judges. Put that constitution out of view, and Lord Tenderden, may be dismissed in the same way as his predecessor Lord Coke was, in the time of James the first.

"Captain Hall has sad misgivings; he tells us as to what will be our fate if the supreme court should at any time falter in its duty, and consent to execute an unconstitutional law. Now there is, of course, no end to the hypotheses which an ingenious mind may frame as to the effect of derelictions of duty, by any department of a government. The house of commons may, as Paley remarks, "put to death the constitution, by the refusal of the annual grants of money to the support of the necessary functions of government." So may the judiciary commit some suicidal act. We have given to our judges every motive to a high and fearless execution of their trust; the oath to support the constitution,—absolute immunity,—and, on the other hand, the infamy of judicial cowardice. Human precaution can go no further. But where are we if all these securities prove ineffectual? Just where other countries are which do not intrust to the judge the power of canvassing a legislative act. What was the history of our revolution? Whilst we were a part of the British empire, an attempt was made to tax us in defiance of a common law principle. As the courts stood ready to enforce these odious measures, we were driven to arms. Lord Chatham declared us to be in the right. Mr Fox has subsequently placed on record his opinion that our resistance preserved the integrity of the English constitution, and parliament itself has recognised the justice of our course by a definition of the true colonial principle. Our present position is this:—we have placed our judges in a situation far more independent than the same functionaries enjoy in England. We are a patient, quiet people, and will submit to a great deal even of what we deem injustice, rather than put all these blessings in peril by violence: but, finally, we hold in reserve for intolerable grievances what Blackstone describes, even in England, as the last resort.

"It is the more to be regretted that Captain Hall should have exhibited an absurd ignorance on this subject, as he has thereby diminished materially the chance of our profiting by his criticism, even when better founded. A foreigner is often struck by errors to which the people, amongst whom they exist, are rendered insensible, and his candid and temperate exposure of them may lead to a reformation, which might have been struggled for in vain by those whose motives were more liable to suspicion. Thus, he very justly denounces the practice, in a few of the states, of rendering the judges periodically elective, thinking that they are thereby exposed to, at least, a suspicion of servility to the government. He thinks that they ought to be placed on the same footing with the judges of the United States, and of the largest states; but unfortunately he has thrown away all his influence as an auxiliary, by seriously pretending to refer these misguided people, in the most triumphant manner, to the case of *England*, when they are too well aware that an evil of the same character exists in that country, in a form infinitely more odious and alarming, and on a scale altogether stupendous.

"The allusion is, of course, to the high court of chancery. There is a sum at stake in the litigation of that court—nay, actually locked up awaiting its decisions—equal to the value of the fee-simple of the states in question, and all their movables into the bargain—a sum more than sufficient to pay off the whole national debt of the United States several times over. Its jurisdiction is of the most diffusive character, and it may be said to reach in some way, either directly or indirectly, the interests or the sympathies of every individual in the community. As no court presents so many temptations to indirect practices, so there is no one in which they may be so readily veiled. A year's *delay*, to obtain which might be an object of sufficient importance to warrant an enormous bribe, would scarcely excite even suspicion in a court whose procrastinating temper is proverbial. There is no jury to participate in its labours, or to check an improper bias; nor do its proceedings possess that kind of popular interest which attracts to them the supervision even of the readers of the newspapers. What is the tenure by which this almost boundless power over the anxieties and the interests of the community is held? The will of the minister of the day: his breath can make or unmake the lord chancellor. A premier would instantly resign if his declared wish for the removal of this officer should be disregarded: such a refusal would be considered as depriving him of an authority essential to the discipline of the cabinet, and to that concert and cordiality on which the success of its measures must so greatly depend. When it is recollected that within the brief space of nine months, there stood at the head of affairs in Great Britain *four* different individuals in succession (Lord Liverpool, Mr Canning, Lord Goderich, the Duke of Wellington), it will readily be conceded that the chancellor can never consider himself as altogether safe, since he is liable to be sacrificed, not merely to any particular scheme of policy, which he is accused of thwarting, but even to those impulses of temper, on the one side or the other, through which Mr Huskisson ceased to be a minister. It seems to be universally agreed that Lord Lyndhurst must have gone out, as the attorney-general did, had he not voted for the Relief Bill of last session.

"If we look back to the history of this court we shall see plainly what has been the practical consequence of this state of things. The mind involuntarily turns to Lord Bacon: the 'greatest, wisest' of mankind, he became lord chancellor only to furnish to the poet a sad antithesis to these epithets. There is nowhere to be found a more mortifying rebuke to the pride of human nature than is furnished in witnessing the influence of circumstances over a mind so wholly without a parallel in modern times, whether we refer to original power and compass, or to extent of acquirement. His appointment, as appears by his own letters, was brought about by Buckingham, the favourite of King James. The abject subjection in which he was held is thus stated by his biographer *Mallet*. 'During the king's absence in Scotland, there happened an affair, otherwise of small importance, but as it lets us into the true genius of those times, and serves to show in what miserable subjection the favourite held all those who were in public employments. He was on the point of ruining Sir Francis Bacon, the person he had just contributed to raise; not for any error or negligence in their master's service, but merely for an opinion given in a thing that only regarded his own family. Indeed, such was his levity, such the insolence of his power, that the capricious removal of men from their places became the prime distinction of his thirteen years' favour, which, as Bishop Hacket observes, was like a sweeping flood that at every spring-tide takes from one land to cast what it has taken upon another.' And again, 'nor even thus did he presently regain his credit with Buckingham; the family continued to load him with reproaches: and he remained long under *that agony of heart which an aspiring man must feel* when his power and dignity are at the mercy of a king's minion, young and giddy with his elevation. They were, however, reconciled at last, and their friendship, *if obsequiousness in one, to all the humours of the other, deserves* the name of friendship, continued without interruption for some years; while Buckingham went on daily to place and displace the great officers of the crown, as wantonness of fancy, or anger, or interest led him; *to recommend or discountenance every private person, who had a suit depending in any court just as he was influenced;* to authorise and protect every illegal project that could serve most speedily to enrich himself or his kindred,' &c.

"At length his bribery and venality became so flagrant and notorious, that it was found necessary to put him aside.

"What brought about the dismissal of Lord Clarendon from the same high office? We are told that the gravity of his deportment 'struck a very unpleasing awe into a court filled with licentious persons of both sexes;' certain false suggestions were in consequence got up, which, 'assisted by the *solicitations of the ladies of pleasure*, made such impressions upon the king, that he at last gave way and became willing, and even pleased, to part both from his person and services.' (*Chalmers's Biographical Dictionary, art. Hyde.*) *Pepys,* secretary to the admiralty, in the reign of Charles II. thus refers, in his *Diary,* recently edited by Lord Braybrooke, to the same transaction. 'This day, Mr Pierce, the surgeon, was with me; and tells me how this business of my lord chancellor's was certainly designed in my Lady Castlemain's chamber; and that when he went from the king on Monday morning she was in bed (though about twelve o'clock), and ran out in her smock into her aviary, looking into Whitehall-garden; and thither her woman brought her her night-gown, and stood blessing herself at the old man's going away.'

"Clarendon's integrity could not be overcome. Had he proved weak as Lord Bacon, he would have been drawn into the same wretched thraldom to the male or female favourite of the hour. Influence, wherever lodged, would have been an object of dread; and the power of alarming the anxieties of the chancellor have proved the best perquisite of the king's mistress. A magistrate thus debased would quickly come to understand that he might give as much offence by an honest decree as by the gravity of his deportment, and even should an exposure ultimately take place, it would be impossible to trace the taint of corruption through the vast and complicated business of the court, much less to redress the mischief which had been done.

"Coming into the next century, we find Lord Chancellor *the Earl of Macclesfield*, disgraced for bribery and venality.

"The circumstances which more recently led to the dismissal of *Lord Camden* are thus stated by the Earl of Chatham, in his speech explanatory of the pension granted to that illustrious magistrate, *prior* to his appointment as chancellor. (*See Gentleman's Magazine for* 1770, *p.* 104.) 'I recommended him to be chancellor; his public and private virtues were acknowledged by all; *they made his situation more precarious.* I could not reasonably expect from him that he should quit the chief-justiceship of the common pleas, which he held for life, and *put himself in the power* of those who were not to be trusted, *to be dismissed from the chancery, perhaps the day after his appointment.* The public has not been deceived by his conduct. My suspicions have been justified. *His integrity has made him once more a poor and a private man;* he was dismissed for the vote he gave in favour of the right of election in the subject.' In the same volume, p. 141, will be found 'The Humble Address, Remonstrance, and Petition of the Electors of the City and Liberty of Westminster, assembled in Westminster-hall, the 28th March 1770,' in which they say, 'by the same *secret and unhappy influence to which all our grievances have been originally owing*, the redress of those grievances has been now prevented; and the grievances themselves have been repeatedly confirmed, with this additional circumstance of aggravation, that *while the invaders of our rights* remain the *directors of your majesty's counsels*, the defenders of those rights have been dismissed from your majesty's service, your majesty having been advised by your ministers to remove from his employment for his vote in parliament the highest officer of the law, because his principles suited ill with theirs, and *his pure* distribution of justice with *their corrupt* administration of it in the house of commons.'

"Whilst, therefore, the great law officer of England sits at the council board, and at the banquet, with the sword suspended over his head by a single hair—whilst in the middle of a cause he may learn that his judicial functions are at an end—Captain Hall, with a generous waiver of all selfish considerations, thinks only of the poor souls on the other side of the Atlantic.

'Woe, woe, for Indiana, not a whit for me!'

"His sympathies are on a mission to the Ohio, to awaken people *there* to a sense of their perilous condition, whilst his own brethren are left unheeded behind. He dreads lest in the legislature of some one of the states composed of men 'who have come straight from the plough, or from behind the counter, from chopping down trees, or from the bar,' corruption may be found. He has no fear of the abuse of power by an individual."

*General Table of all Religious Denominations throughout the United States, specifying the number of Ministers, Churches, Communicants, and Individuals.*

| Denominations. | Ministers. | Churches, or Congregations. | Communicants. | Population. |
|---|---|---|---|---|
| 1. Calvinistic Baptists | 2,914 | 4,384 | 304,827 | 2,743,453 |
| 2. Methodist Episcopal Church | 1,777 | | 476,000 | 2,600,000 |
| 3. Presbyterians (General Assembly) | 1,801 | 2,253 | 182,017 | 1,800,000 |
| 4. Congregationalists (orthodox) | 1,000 | 1,270 | 140,000 | 1,260,000 |
| 5. Protestant Episcopal Church | 558 | 700 | | 600,000 |
| 6. Universalists | 150 | 300 | | 500,000 |
| 7. Roman Catholics | | | | 500,000 |
| 8. Lutherans | 205 | 1,200 | 44,000 | 400,000 |
| *9. Christians | 200 | 800 | 25,000 | 275,000 |
| 10. German Reformed | 84 | 400 | 17,400 | 200,000 |
| 11. Friends, or Quakers | | 400 | | 200,000 |
| 12. Unitarians (Congregationalists) | 160 | 193 | | 176,000 |
| 13. Associate and other Methodists | 350 | | 35,000 | 175,000 |
| 14. Free-will Baptists | 300 | 400 | 16,000 | 150,000 |
| 15. Dutch Reformed | 159 | 194 | 17,888 | 125,000 |
| 16. Mennonites | 200 | | 30,000 | 120,000 |
| 17. Associate Presbyterians | 74 | 144 | 15,000 | 100,000 |
| 18. Cumberland Presbyterians | 50 | 75 | 8,000 | 100,000 |
| 19. Tunkers, or Dunkers | 40 | 40 | 3,000 | 30,000 |
| 20. Free-communion Baptists | 30 | | 3,500 | 30,000 |
| 21. Seventh-day Baptists | 30 | 40 | 2,000 | 20,000 |
| 22. Six-principle Baptists | 25 | 30 | 1,800 | 20,000 |
| 23. United Brethren, or Moravians | 23 | 23 | 2,000 | 7,000 |
| 24. Millenial Church, or Shakers | 45 | 15 | | 6,000 |
| 25. New Jerusalem Church | 30 | 28 | | 5,000 |
| 26. Emancipators (Baptists) | 15 | | 600 | 4,500 |
| 27. Jews and others not mentioned, Sandemanians | | 150 | | 50,000 |

N.B. Lists of many more than double the above number of sects and denominations as existing in England and elsewhere, are given by Evans, Hannah More, Hulbert, &c.; but these are all that are mentioned by the "American Almanac," for 1832 (a most useful work published at Boston); "Quarterly Register of American Education;" "Sword's Ecclesiastical Register;" "Report of American Unitarian Association," &c. &c. on which authorities the above table is given.—W. G. O.

*General Bernard's Comparative Statement*

FRENCH BUDGET.

| | | Francs. | Francs. |
|---|---|---|---|
| Public Debt | . . . . | | 247,943,065 |
| Civil List | . . . . | | 32,000,000 |
| Justice | . . | 19,097,020 | |
| *Administration Centrale* | . | 552,000 | |
| | Total | | 19,649,020 |
| Foreign Affairs | . | 8,180,000 | |
| *Administration Centrale* | . | 820,000 | |
| | Total | | 9,000,000 |
| *Interieur*, or Home Department. | | | |
| *Ponts et chaussées, mines, travaux publics, lignes telegraphique*, &c. | | 91,513,517 | |
| Miscellaneous | . . | 12,935,483 | |
| *Administration Centrale* | . | 1,151,000 | |
| | Total | | 105,600,000 |
| Ecclesiastical Affairs | . | 35,551,500 | |
| *Administration Centrale* | . | 370,000 | |
| | Total | | 35,921,500 |
| Public Instruction | . . . | | 1,995,000 |
| Commerce and Manufactures | | 2,844,000 | |
| *Administration Centrale* | . | 450,200 | |
| | Total | | 3,294,200 |

*of the French and American Budgets.*

AMERICAN BUDGET.

| | Francs. | Cs. | Francs. | Cs. |
|---|---|---|---|---|
| Public Debt . . . | | | 52,500,000 | 00 |
| Civil List . . . | | | 131,250 | 00 |
| Department of State . . | 3,179,101 | 69 | | |
| Central Administration . . | 170,409 | 75 | | |
| Total | | | 3,349,511 | 44 |

| | | Francs. | Francs. |
|---|---|---|---|
| War Department . . | | 185,623,000 | |
| *Administration Centrale* . | | 1,577,000 | |
| | Total | ——— | 187,200,000 |
| *Marine*, or Naval Department | | 64,480,000 | |
| *Administration Centrale* . | | 790,000 | |
| | Total | ——— | 65,270,000 |
| Finance . . . | | 94,954,100 | |
| *Administration Centrale* . | | 5,000,000 | |
| | Total | ——— | 99,954,100 |
| Post Office . . | | 14,546,294 | |
| *Administration Centrale* . | | 2,233,530 | |
| | Total | ——— | 16,779,824 |
| Administration of Public Revenues | | 108,388,268 | |
| Central Administration . | | 3,000,955 | |
| (Without the Post Office) | Total | ——— | 111,389,223 |
| Reimbursements and Compensations | | . | 49,939,397 |
| Total of French Budget . | | . | 977,935,329 |

Or (at 25 francs) about £39,117,413

| | Francs. | Cs. | Francs. | Cs. |
|---|---|---|---|---|
| War Department | | | | |
| Army, Fortifications, and Matériel of Artillery . | 20,601,943 | 47 | | |
| Public Works . . | 4,454,748 | 06 | | |
| Indians . . | 2,749,725 | 14 | | |
| Central Administration . | 327,429 | 38 | | |
| Total | | | 28,133,846 | 05 |
| Naval Department . | 22,466,660 | 21 | | |
| Central Administration . | 247,112 | 25 | | |
| Total | | | 22,713,772 | 46 |
| Treasury Department . | 21,911,335 | 85 | | |
| Central Administration . | 1,369,987 | 50 | | |
| Total | | | 23,281,323 | 35 |
| Post Office . . . | | | 321,772 | 50 |
| (This is not a branch of public revenue in the United States; the receipts cover the expenditure, all but the mere expenses of office or Administration Centrale.) | | | | |
| Total of American Budget . | | | 130,431,475 | 80 |

Or (at 25 francs) £5,217,259

*Table showing the number of Clergymen and Churches of different Denominations in each State of the Union, as far as they have been ascertained.*

N.B. The spaces marked ? denote that there are clergymen and churches of the particular sect, but their number not known. Those Nos. marked thus, 20*, are doubtful. Among the ministers are reckoned also the licentiates. For further details consult General Table, page 207.

| States and Territories, &c. of the Union. | Protestant Episcopal. | | Presbyterians. | | Roman Catholics. | | German Reformed. | | Unitarians. | | | | Baptists. | | Dutch Reformed. | | | | | Congregationalists. | | | | |
|---|---|---|---|---|---|---|---|---|---|---|---|---|---|---|---|---|---|---|---|---|---|---|---|---|
| | Clergymen. | Churches. | Ministers. | Churches. | Clergymen. | Churches. | Clergymen. | Churches. | Ministers. | Societies or Churches. | Friends or Quakers' Societies | *Methodists.* Ministers. | Ministers and Licentiates. | Churches & Associations | Clergymen. | Churches. | Lutherans. | *New Jerusalem Church.* Societies. | *Millenial Church or Shakers.* Ministers. | Pastors. | Churches. | *Free-will Baptists.* Churches or Congregations. | *Christians.*† Ministers. | *Universalists.* Congregate Societies. |
| Maine | 4 | ? | | | ? | 4 | | | 8 | 12 | 30 | 56 | 158 | 210 | | | | 3 | | 107 | 156 | 50 | | ? |
| New Hampshire | 8 | ? | 9 | 11 | ? | 2 | | | 10 | ? | 13 | 30 | 61 | 75 | | | | | 2 | 116 | 146 | 67 | 17 | 20 |
| Vermont | 15 | ? | | | ? | | | | 1 | 3 | | 44 | 64 | 105 | | | | | | 155 | 216 | ? | ? | ? |
| Massachusetts | 31 | ? | 9 | ? | ? | 4 | | | 118 | 100* | | 71 | 110 | 129 | | | | 8 | 4 | 305* | 391 | | | 46 |
| Rhode Island | 59 | ? | | | ? | 1 | | | 2 | 2 | ? | 10 | 12 | 16 | | | | | | 10 | 10 | 8 | | ? |
| Connecticut | | | | | ? | 1 | | | ? | 2 | ? | 40 | 92 | 99 | | | | | 1 | 272 | ? | ? | | ? |
| New York | 129 | ? | 610 | 587 | ? | ? | | | 2 | 5 | ? | 372 | 387 | ? | 118 | 148 | 27 | | ? | | | | | ? |
| New Jersey | 20 | ? | 108 | 85 | | | | | | | ? | 100* | 21 | 34 | 28 | 28 | | | | ? | ? | | | |
| Pennsylvania | 60 | ? | 248 | 429 | ? | ? | 73 | 282 | 3 | 5 | ? | 140 | 96 | 144 | 6 | 6 | 2 | | | 18 | 39 | | | ? |
| Delaware | 6 | ? | 9 | 9 | | | | | | | | 15 | 9 | 9 | | | | | | | | | | |
| ‡Maryland | 57 | ? | 17 | ? | ? | 35* | 9 | ? | ? | 1 | ? | ? | 12 | 15 | | | | 1 | | | | | | |

| | | | | | | | | | | | | | | | | | | | | | | | | |
|---|---|---|---|---|---|---|---|---|---|---|---|---|---|---|---|---|---|---|---|---|---|---|---|---|
| Virginia | 45 | ? | 90 | 104 | ? | ? | | | | | | 77 | 192 | 337 | | | ? | | | | | | | |
| North Carolina | 11 | ? | 66 | 126 | | | | | | | ? | 32 | 139 | 272 | | | 45 | | | ? | 14 | 4 | | |
| South Carolina | 34 | ? | 52 | 77 | ? | ? | | | ? | ? | | 54 | 137 | 159 | | | ? | | | ? | ? | | | |
| Georgia | 4 | 4 | 31 | 55 | 3 | 3 | | | | | ? | 64 | 205 | 390 | | | ? | | | | | 12 | 28 | |
| Alabama | 2 | ? | 33 | 38 | 9 | ? | | | | | | 44 | 130 | 219 | | | | | | | | 12 | | |
| Mississippi | 4 | ? | 24 | 25 | ? | ? | | | | | | 23 | 15 | 58 | | | | | | | | ? | | |
| §Louisiana | 3 | ? | 5 | 3 | ? | 20* | | | | | | 6 | 15 | 28 | | | | | | | | ? | | |
| ‖Tennessee | 5 | ? | 80 | 105 | | | | | | | | 125 | 141 | 214 | | | 10 | | | | | 11 | | |
| Kentucky | | | 70 | 103 | 30 | ? | | | | | | 77 | 290 | 442 | | | | | | | | 25 | | |
| Ohio | 16 | ? | 203 | 346 | ? | ? | ? | 82 | ? | ? | ? | 91 | 140 | 240 | | | 37 | 4 | ? | 20 | 65 | 14 | | ? |
| Indiana | | | 20 | 50 | | | | | | | | 34 | 130 | 181 | | | | | | | | 11 | | |
| Illinois | | | 13 | 24 | | | | | | | | 45 | 70 | 80 | | | | | | | | 6 | | |
| Missouri | 3 | ? | 10 | 17 | ? | ? | | | | | | 23 | 67 | 111 | | | | | | | | 9 | | |
| District of Columbia | 5 | ? | 16 | 9 | ? | ? | | | 1 | 1* | | 14* | 10 | 18 | | | | | | | | | | |
| Territory of Michigan | 5 | ? | 6 | 6 | ? | ? | | | | | | 11 | 2 | ? | | | | | | | | 1 | | |
| Territory of Arkansas | 1 | ? | 4* | ? | ? | ? | | | | | | 7 | 2 | 8 | | | | | | | | 1 | | |
| Territory of Florida | | | | | | | | | | | | | | | | | | | | | | | | |

Besides these, there are United Brethren, Associate Presbyterians, Evangelical Lutherans, Sandemanians, Jews, &c., and Indians, whom it is difficult to classify, but they are not generally numerous.

† Christ-ians, a peculiar sect. They pronounce their distinctive denomination as a dipthong—*Chreist*-ians.

‡ In Maryland, the greater portion of the inhabitants are Roman Catholics. The Roman Catholic archbishop resides in this state, and is the Metropolitan of the United States.

§ The Roman Catholics are the most numerous religious denomination in Louisiana. The whole state is divided into twenty *ecclesiastical* parishes; but I have not been able to obtain exact returns of the number of churches or priests.

‖ *Cumberland Presbyterians*, about 100,000, reside chiefly in Tennessee and Kentucky.—W. G. O.

*Table, showing the Governor's Term and Salary, the number of Senators and Representatives, with their respective Terms and Pay in the different States.*

| States. | Govr's term of years. | Salary. | Senators. | Term of years. | Representatives. | Term of years. | Total of sen. & rep. | Pay per day in dollars. | Expense of one month for sen. and rep. |
|---|---|---|---|---|---|---|---|---|---|
| Maine | 1 | 1500 | 20 | 1 | 153 | 1 | 173 | 2.00 | 10,380 |
| New Hampshire | 1 | 1200 | 12 | 1 | 229 | 1 | 236 | 2.00 | 14,160 |
| Vermont* | 1 | 750 | none | | 230 | 1 | 230 | 1.50 | 10,350 |
| Massachusetts† | 1 | 5666⅔ | 40 | 1 | 481 | | 521 | 2.00 | 31,260 |
| Rhode Island | 1 | 400 | 10 | 1 | 72 | ½ | 82 | 1.50 | 3,690 |
| Connecticut‡ | 1 | 1100 | 21 | 1 | 208 | 1 | 229 | 2.00 | 13,740 |
| New York | 2 | 4000 | 32 | 4 | 128 | 1 | 160 | 3.00 | 1,440 |
| New Jersey§ | 1 | 2000 | 14 | 1 | 50 | 1 | 64 | 3.00 | 5,760 |
| Pennsylvania | 3 | 4000 | 33 | 4 | 100 | 1 | 133 | 3.00 | 10,970 |
| Delaware | 3 | 1333⅓ | 9 | 3 | 21 | 1 | 30 | 2.50 | 2,250 |
| Maryland | 1 | 3500 | 15 | 5 | 80 | 1 | 95 | 4.00 | 11,400 |
| Virginia | 3 | 3333⅓ | 32 | 4 | 134 | 1 | 166 | 4.00 | 19,920 |
| North Carolina | 1 | 2000 | 64 | 1 | 134 | 1 | 198 | 3.00 | 17,820 |
| South Carolina | 2 | 3900 | 45 | 4 | 124 | 2 | 169 | 4.00 | 20,280 |
| Georgia | 2 | 3000 | 78 | 1 | 142 | 1 | 220 | 4.00 | 26,400 |
| Alabama | 2 | 2000 | 22 | 3 | 72 | | 94 | 4.00 | 11,280 |
| Mississippi | 2 | 2500 | 11 | 3 | 36 | 1 | 47 | 3.00 | 4,230 |
| Louisiana | 4 | 7500 | 17 | 4 | 50 | 2 | 67 | 4.00 | 7,040 |
| Tennessee | 2 | 2000 | 20 | 2 | 60 | 2 | 80 | 4.00 | 9,600 |
| Kentucky | 4 | 2000 | 38 | 4 | 100 | 1 | 138 | 2.00 | 8,280 |
| Ohio | 2 | 1200 | 36 | 2 | 72 | 1 | 108 | 3.00 | 9,720 |
| Indiana | 3 | 1000 | 23 | 3 | 62 | 1 | 85 | 2.00 | 5,100 |
| Illinois | 4 | 1000 | ? | 4 | ? | 2 | ? | 3.00 | ? |
| Missouri | 4 | 1500 | 18 | 4 | 49 | 2 | 65 | 3.00 | 5,940 |
| | | 56,383⅓ ‖ dollars, or about 12,600*l*. | | | | | Total ¶ | | 261,010 |

or, allowing 6,000 dollars for Illinois, not ascertained, 267,010 dollars.

* There is no senate in the legislature of Vermont; but the executive council, consisting of the governor, lieutenant governor, and twelve counsellors, elected by the freemen, are empowered to lay before the general assembly such business as shall appear to them necessary; also to revise and propose amendments to the laws passed by the house of representatives.

† The number of representatives in the legislature of Massachusetts in 1831 was 481; but the number is very variable.

‡ The pay of the *senators*, in the legislature of Connecticut, is two dollars a day, that of the *representatives* 1.50.

§ The upper house, which forms an independent branch of the legislature of New Jersey, is styled the "Legislative Council."

‖ These salaries appear very low; but it must be remarked, that the post of governor of a state is less one of emolument than of distinction and power; the expense it entails generally greatly exceeding the amount of salary. It is somewhat analogous, in this respect, to the lord-lieutenantcies of counties in this country.

¶ A small allowance per mile is made for the travelling expenses of the members of the legislature, the exact aggregate amount of which sums it would be difficult to calculate: by allowing a session of nearly five months in the year, in all the states, we certainly cover this expense.

From the above table it will appear that the total amount of the sums paid to the senators and representatives of the *state legislatures* throughout the whole union, together with the salaries of the governors, would not amount to 280,000*l*. English, if all the legislatures were to remain in session between four and five months in the year (the average is perhaps not more than two or three months, in reality).—W. G. O.

*Statement, showing the aggregate number of persons in each of the States, according to the fifth census, and distinguishing the Slave from the Free Population in each State, according to the corrections made in the returns of the Marshals and their assistants by the Secretary of State.*

(From Letter of Secretary of State to Speaker of House of Representatives, dated Jan 4, 1832.)

| States. | Number of white persons. | Number of free colored. | Total of free persons. | Slaves. | Total of all descriptions. |
|---|---|---|---|---|---|
| Maine | 398,260 | 1,171 | 399,431 | 6 | 399,437 |
| New Hampshire | 268,721 | 602 | 269,323 | 5 | 269,328 |
| Massachusetts | 603,359 | 7,045 | 610,404 | 4 | 610,408 |
| Rhode Island | 93,621 | 3,564 | 97,185 | 14 | 97,199 |
| Connecticut | 289,603 | 8,047 | 297,650 | 25 | 297,675 |
| Vermont | 279,776 | 881 | 280,657 | none | 280,657 |
| New York | 1,868,061 | 44,869 | 1,912,930 | 76 | 1,913,006 *125 |
| New Jersey | 300,266 | 18,303 | 318,569 | 2,254 | 320,823 |
| Pennsylvania | 1,309,900 | 37,930 | 1,347,830 | 403 | 1,348,233 |
| Delaware | 57,601 | 15,855 | 73,456 | 3,292 | 76,748 |
| Maryland | 291,108 | 52,938 | 344,046 | 102,994 | 447,040 |
| Virginia | 694,300 | 47,348 | 741,648 | 469,757 | 1,211,405 |
| North Carolina | 472,843 | 19,543 | 492,386 | 245,601 | 737,987 |
| South Carolina | 257,863 | 7,921 | 265,784 | 315,401 | 581,185 |
| Georgia | 296,806 | 2,486 | 299,292 | 217,531 | 516,823 |
| Alabama | 190,406 | 1,572 | 191,978 | 117,549 | 309,527 |
| Mississippi | 70,443 | 519 | 70,962 | 65,659 | 136,621 |
| Louisiana | 89,231 | 16,710 | 105,941 | 109,588 | 215,529 *210 |
| Tennessee | 535,746 | 4,555 | 540,301 | 141,603 | 681,904 |
| Kentucky | 517,787 | 4,917 | 522,704 | 165,213 | 687,917 |
| Ohio | 926,311 | 9,567 | 935,878 | 6 | 935,884 |
| Indiana | 339,399 | 3,629 | 343,028 | 3 | 343,031 |
| Illinois | 115,061 | 1,637 | 156,698 | 747 | 157,445 |
| Missouri | 114,795 | 569 | 115,364 | 25,091 | 140,455 |

* Aliens, or persons not classified under the above heads.

N.B. It will be perceived that the population returns for the territories of Florida, Arkansa and Michigan, and the district of Columbia, being wanting, no total is here given of the whole population of the United States, which probably amounts, however, to, at present, as nearly as possible, 13,000,000. In 1830 the census gave 12,856,165 as the total population.—W. G. O.

## STEAM-BOAT NAVIGATION FROM ST LOUIS.

St Louis is 1200 miles, by the course of the river, above New Orleans, and is, next to that city, the largest and most commercial town on the Mississippi. In the summer of 1831 there were six steam-boats regularly employed between St Louis and New Orleans. A trip from one place to the other, and back again, usually occupies twenty-four days; the shortest time in which one was ever made, eighteen days. The usual fare for cabin passengers descending, 20 dollars; ascending, 25 dollars; for deck passengers, 5 dollars, either way. Freight per 100 lbs. descending, 37½ cents; ascending, 62½ cents.

From St Louis to Louisville, 630 miles; six boats regularly running, in 1831; usual time of a trip ten or eleven days; the passage one way usually being somewhat more than three days: fare of cabin passengers about 15 dollars, either way; deck passengers 4 dollars: freight about 25 cents per 100 lb. One boat also ran regularly to Cincinnati, 150 miles above Louisville.

From St Louis to Fever River, about 480 miles, three steam-boats regularly employed in 1831; time occupied by a trip about ten days: fare for passengers ascending, 15 dollars; descending, 9 dollars. The route of one of the boats occasionally extended to St Peter's River, 400 miles further up.

In 1821 two boats were employed in running from St Louis up the Missouri to Franklin, 200 miles, and to Fort Leavenworth, 200 miles further: freight to Franklin 75 cents per 100 lbs., and to Fort Leavenworth from 1.25 to 1.50 dollars: from Franklin down, 25 cents per 100 lbs.

From St Louis to Pekin, on Illinois River, 180 miles: two or three boats regularly employed in 1831. Steam-boats come occasionly to St Louis, from Pittsburg and other places.

*Whole number of Steam Boats built on the Western Waters.*

| When built. | Whole number. | Now running. | Lost or worn out. | Of the Boats now running, | | |
|---|---|---|---|---|---|---|
| 1811 | 1 | | 1 | 68 | were built at | Cincinnati |
| 1814 | 4 | | 4 | 68 | .... | Pittsburgh |
| 1815 | 3 | | 3 | 2 | ... | Louisville |
| 1816 | 2 | | 2 | 12 | .... | New Albany |
| 1817 | 9 | | 9 | 7 | .... | Marietta |
| 1818 | 23 | | 23 | 2 | .... | Zanesville |
| 1819 | 27 | | 27 | 1 | .... | Fredericksburgh |
| 1820 | 7 | 1 | 6 | 1 | .... | Westport |
| 1821 | 6 | 1 | 5 | 1 | .... | Silver Creek |
| 1822 | 7 | | 7 | 1 | .... | Brush Creek |
| 1823 | 13 | 1 | 12 | 2 | .... | Wheeling |
| 1824 | 13 | 1 | 12 | 1 | .... | Nashville |
| 1825 | 31 | 19 | 12 | 2 | .... | Frankfort |
| 1826 | 52 | 36 | 16 | 1 | .... | Smithland |
| 1827 | 25 | 19 | 6 | 1 | .... | Economy |
| 1828 | 31 | 28 | 3 | 6 | .... | Brownsville |
| 1829 | 53 | 53 | | 3 | .... | Portsmouth |
| 1830 | 30 | 30 | | 2 | .... | Steubenville |
| 1831 | 9 | 9 | | 2 | .... | Beaver |
| | | | | 1 | .... | St Louis |
| | | | | 3 | .... | New York |
| | | | | 1 | .... | Philadelphia |
| | | | | 10 | .... | Not known |
| | 348 | 198 | 150* | 198† | | |

* Of the 150 lost or worn out, there were:—

| | |
|---|---|
| Worn out . . . . | 63 |
| Lost by "snags" . . . | 36 |
| Burnt . . . . | 14 |
| Lost by collision . . . | 3 |
| By other accidents, not ascertained | 24 |
| Total | 150 |

† Of this whole number, 111 were built at Cincinnati, 68 of which were running in 1831.

*Expenses to each State of its Judiciary, including the Territories and District of Columbia.*

| | Dollars. | | Dollars. |
|---|---|---|---|
| Maine | 10,000 | Georgia** | 16,800 |
| New Hampshire | 7,800 | Alabama | 12,250 |
| Vermont, about | 6,000 | Mississippi | 12,000 |
| Massachusetts | 29,800 | Louisiana, about | 20,000 |
| Rhode Island,* about | 2,000 | Tennessee | 22,700 |
| Connecticut† | 6,158 | Kentucky†† | 20,900 |
| New York‡ | 26,500 | Ohio‡‡ | 13,800 |
| New Jersey | 3,400 | Indiana§§ | 7,000 |
| Pennsylvania§ | 50,666 | Illinois | 4,700 |
| Delaware | 5,500 | Missouri | 8,300 |
| Maryland | 23,000 | District of Columbia‖‖ | 9,000 |
| Virginia‖ | 12,720 | Florida | 6,000 |
| North Carolina¶ | 12,900 | Michigan | 6,000 |
| South Carolina | 34,072 | Arkansas | 6,000 |
| | 230,416 | | 165,450 |

Total . 395,866 Dollars.

* In Rhode Island some of the judges are paid by fees.

† In Connecticut county courts the chief judges have three and a half dollars per diem; associate judges, three dollars during session, and nine cents per mile for their journeys.

‡ In New York, the registers, reporters, and clerks of Chancery and Superior Courts are paid by fees.

§ In Pennsylvania, the prothonotaries paid by fees; judges of Superior Courts, when travelling, four dollars per diem.

‖ In Virginia, the judges receive one quarter of a dollar per mile, for travelling, additional.

¶ In North Carolina there are some fees.

** In Georgia some fees.

†† In Kentucky there are some fees.

‡‡ In Ohio there are fees, and associate judges in each county court receive two and a half dollars per diem during courts.

§§ In Indiana, the associates get two dollars per diem.

‖‖ In the district of Columbia there are fees also.—W. G. O.

## *Colleges in the United States.*

| Name. | Place. | When founded. | Instructors. | Number of Alumni. | Number of Ministers. | Students†. |
|---|---|---|---|---|---|---|
| Bowdoin | Brunswick, Maine | 1794 | 7 | 392 | 39 | 137 |
| Waterville | Waterville, Do | 1820 | 5 | 60 | 19 | 45 |
| Dartmouth | Hanover N. Hampshire | 1770 | 9 | 2250 | 530 | 153 |
| University of Vermont | Burlington, Vermont | 1791 | 4 | 182 | | 36 |
| Middlebury | Middlebury, Do | 1800 | 5 | 509 | 205 | 99 |
| Harward University | Cambridge, Massachusetts | 1638 | 24 | 5621 | 1424 | 236 |
| Williams | Williamstown, Do | 1793 | 7 | 721 | 215 | 115 |
| Amherst | Amherst, Do | 1821 | 10 | 208 | 52 | 188 |
| Brown University | Providence, Rhode Island | 1764 | 6 | 1182 | 442 | 95 |
| Yale | New Haven, Connecticut | 1700 | 15 | 4428 | 1257 | 346 |
| Washington | Hartford, Do | 1826 | 9 | 25 | | 70 |
| Wesleyan University | Middletown, Do | 1831 | 5 | | | |
| Columbia | New York, New York | 1754 | 6 | 880 | | 124 |
| Union | Schenectady, Do | 1795 | 10 | 1373 | 268 | 205 |
| Hamilton | Clinton, Do | 1812 | 7 | 189 | 20 | 77 |
| Geneva | Geneva, Do | 1823 | 6 | 15 | 6 | 31 |
| College of New Jersey | Princeton, New Jersey | 1746 | 10 | 1930 | 406 | 105 |
| Rutgers | New Brunswick, Do | 1770 | 5 | | | 70 |
| University of Pennsylvania | Philadelphia, Pennsylvania | 1755 | 9 | | | 125 |
| Dickinson | Carlisle, Do | 1783 | 4 | | | 21 |
| Jefferson | Canonsburg, Do | 1802 | 7 | 341 | 136 | 120 |
| Western University | Pittsburg, Do | 1820 | 4 | 45 | 13 | 53 |
| Washington | Washington, Do | 1806 | 4 | 143 | 26 | 47 |
| Allegheny | Meadville, Do | 1815 | 3 | 9 | | 6 |
| Madison | Union Town, Do | 1829 | 5 | | | 70 |
| St Mary's* | Baltimore, Maryland | 1799 | 18 | | | 147 |
| University of Maryland | Do Do | 1812 | 11 | | | |
| St Johns | Annapolis, Do | 1784 | 5 | 636 | | 76 |
| Mount St Mary's* | Near Emmittsburg, Do | 1830 | 25 | 12 | | 130 |
| Columbian | Washington, Capital | 1821 | 4 | | | 50 |
| Georgetown* | Georgetown, Dist. Columbia | 1799 | 19 | | | 140 |
| William and Mary | Williamsburg, Virginia | 1693 | 7 | | | 60 |
| Hampden Sydney | Prince Edward Colony, Do | 1774 | 6 | | | 54 |
| Washington | Lexington, Do | 1812 | | 380 | 9 | 23 |
| University of Virginia | Charlottesville, Do | 1819 | 9 | 538 | | 130 |
| University of North Carolina | Chapel Hill, North Carolina | 1791 | 9 | 434 | | 69 |
| Charleston | Charleston, South Carolina | 1785 | 7 | 27 | 3 | 61 |
| College of South Carolina | Columbia, Do | 1801 | 9 | 490 | 11 | 111 |
| University of Georgia | Athens, Georgia | 1785 | 7 | 256 | 16 | 95 |
| Alabama University | Tuscaloosa, Alabama | 1820 | 6 | | | 65 |
| Jefferson | Washington, Mississippi | 1802 | 10 | | | 160 |
| Louisiana | Jackson, Louisiana | | | | | |
| Greenville | Greenville, Tennessee | 1794 | | | | 32 |
| University of Nashville | Nashville, Do | 1806 | 4 | 93 | | 95 |
| E. Tennessee | Knoxville, Do | | 2 | | | 21 |
| Transylvania | Lexington, Kentucky | 1798 | 6 | | | 93 |
| Centre | Danville, Do | 1822 | 4 | 19 | 9 | 66 |
| Augusta | Augusta Do | 1823 | 7 | | | 98 |
| Cumberland | Princeton, Do | 1825 | 3 | 13 | 5 | 57 |
| St Joseph's* | Bardstown, Do | 1819 | 15 | 37 | | 150 |
| Georgetown | Georgetown, Do | 1830 | | | | 32 |
| University of Ohio | Athens, Ohio | 1802 | 4 | 60 | 26 | 57 |
| Miami University | Oxford, Do | 1824 | 11 | 51 | 9 | 82 |
| Western Reserve | Hudson, Do | 1826 | 4 | | | 25 |

*Colleges in the United States.—Continued.*

| Name. | Place. | When founded. | Instructors. | Number of Alumni. | Number of Ministers. | Students†. |
|---|---|---|---|---|---|---|
| Kenyon | Gambier, Do | 1828 | 4 | | | 80 |
| Frankland | New Athens, Do | 1824 | 3 | | | 40 |
| Indiana | Bloomington, Indiana | 1827 | 3 | 4 | | 51 |
| Illinois | Jacksonville, Illinois | 1830 | 3 | | | 35 |
| St Louis* | St Louis, Mo. | 1829 | 6 | | | 125 |

N.B. Besides the Colleges enumerated in the above table, there are upwards of twenty Protestant, and several Catholic "Theological Seminaries," from sixteen to twenty "Medical Schools," and Law Schools in several states.

Each of these institutions possesses a college library and a student's library.

* Those marked thus * are Catholic colleges.

† Under-graduates, not including medical, theological, and law students.

# TEXAS.

This Mexican province, which is now becoming a subject of deep interest in the United States, is of great extent. Its boundaries and superficial contents are thus stated in Darby's Western Gazetteer, published in 1818. The Texas "is bounded on the west and south by the Rio del Porte, on the south by the Gulf of Mexico, east by the state of Louisiana, and north by the Red River. Its greatest length is 800 miles, breadth 500, estimated by the rhombs on Mellish's Map to contain 240,000 square miles, and to be equal in extent to New York, New Jersey, Pennsylvania, Maryland, Virginia, Ohio, and Kentucky."

In another account it is stated, that the width is about 400 miles, and length, from the Gulf of Mexico to its northern limits, not ascertained. It is represented as being extremely fertile, producing a great variety of valuable timber trees, and in parts admirably adapted for the cultivation of sugar, cotton, indigo, &c.; in others, wheat, Indian corn, &c., and in others, excellent grazing, and generally favourable to the growth of the vine.

The facilities for navigation are great; on one side the gulf of Mexico, and the interior traversed by the Sabine, the Natchez, the Trinity, the Brasos, the Bernard, the Colorado, the Rio Grande, and other streams of minor importance. Some of these streams admit of steam navigation for three or four hundred miles. Salt water and iron ore are abundant. Some mines of the precious metals are already discovered. Profusion of game and wild horses, mules and cattle, buffaloes, deer, turkeys, &c.

Its population consists of about 75,000 Mexicans, including garrisons, principally inhabiting the villages of St Antonio and Nacogdoches; but the emigrants from the United States amount to *five or six thousand souls:* more than half of these are "located" on "Austin's land," the remainder principally *occupy ungranted lands.* An experience of seven or eight years has proved the soil and crops to be equal to those of any part of the world.

A writer in one of the best conducted papers in the United States (Walsh's National Gazette) thus significantly expresses himself with regard to the Texas: "The country above described, we contend, should belong to the United States if its procurement be possible." He then gives reasons for supposing its acquisition possible,—the financial embarrassment and unquiet state of the politics of Mexico, &c., and urges as motives for attempting its annexation to the United States, its being necessary to the security of Louisiana, Arkansa, &c. "*All Texas was once ours.* The Rio Grande del Norte was then our western boundary. To any one acquainted with this country, it seems as if this river was *designated by the hand of Heaven, as a boundary* between two great nations of dissimilar pursuits, &c." And further, so important was it deemed by the American government to prevent contiguous settlements of the two governments, that in their negotiation with Spain in 1805, in relation to their western limits, it was urged by the United States to lay off a territory of immense extent, to remain for ever neutral and unsettled. (*See Letter of Messrs Monroe and Pinckney to M. Cevallos, Spanish Minister. American State Papers,* vol. xii. 243.)

It is also urged, that the possession of the Texas is necessary, in order to prevent it from being a place of refuge for "debtors, malefactors, and *fugitive slaves* from the United States;" and that it is necessary, in order to keep Texas out of the hands of "those who would be more troublesome than its present proprietors:" this writer says, that "a distinguished Englishman has already obtained a grant of land in Texas, sufficient to contain a population of one or two millions;" "*and who knows*," adds this sagacious politician, "that he is not the secret agent of a government? The importance, also, of being able to supply the United States with wine and sugar at a future period from this magnificent province, is dwelt upon."

The settlement of Americans in Texas goes by the name of Captain Austin's territory, as that gentleman has obtained a grant, with some exclusive privileges of steam navigation from the Mexican government.

*Payment of the Debt of the United States.*

| | Principal. | Interest. | Total. |
|---|---|---|---|
| | Dollars. | Dollars. | Dollars. |
| 1821 | 3,279,821 | 5,087,272 | 8,367,093 |
| 1822 | 2,675,987 | 5,172,961 | 7,848,949 |
| 1823 | 607,331 | 4,922,684 | 5,530,016 |
| 1824 | 11,574,532 | 4,993,861 | 16,568,393 |
| 1825 | 7,725,034 | 4,370,309 | 12,095,344 |
| 1826 | 7,706,601 | 3,977,864 | 11,045,466 |
| 1827 | 6,515,514 | 3,476,071 | 10,001,585 |
| 1828 | 9,064,637 | 3,098,867 | 12,163,505 |
| 1829 | 9,841,024 | 2,542,776 | 12,383,800 |
| 1830 | 9,443,173 | 1,912,574 | 11,355,748 |

From Mr Cooper's Letter, published in Paris, containing a counter statement to that in the Revue Britannique.

# RATES OF POSTAGE.

On a single letter composed of one piece of paper:—

| | | | |
|---|---|---|---|
| For any distance not exceeding | 30 miles | . . | 6 cents. |
| Over 30, and not exceeding | 80 | . . | 10 |
| 80, " " | 150 | . . | 12½ |
| 150, " " | 400 | . . | 18¾ |
| 400, " " | . . . | . . | 25 |

(A cent is a small fraction more than a half penny, English.)

A letter composed of two pieces of paper is charged with *double* these rates; of three pieces, with *triple;* and of four pieces, with *quadruple.* " One or more pieces of paper, mailed as a letter, and weighing *one ounce*, shall be charged with *quadruple postage;* and at the same rate, should the weight be greater."

## NEWSPAPER POSTAGE.

For each newspaper not carried out of the state in which it is published, or if carried out of the state, but not carried over 100 miles, 1 cent; over 100 miles, and out of the state in which it was published, 1½ cent.

## MAGAZINES AND PAMPHLETS.

| | | | Cents. |
|---|---|---|---|
| If published periodically, distance | not exceeding | 100 miles, | 1½ per sheet. |
| " " . | over . | 100 " | 2½ |
| If not published periodically, dist. | not exceeding | 100 " | 4 |
| " " . | over . | 100 " | 6 |

Every printed pamphlet or magazine which contains more than twenty-four pages, on a *royal* sheet, or any sheet of *less* dimensions, shall be charged by the sheet; and small pamphlets, printed on " a half or quarter sheet, of royal or less size, shall be charged with half the amount of postage charged on a full sheet."

The postage on *ship letters*, if delivered at the office where the vessel arrives, is six cents; if conveyed by post, two cents in addition to the ordinary postage.

## PRIVILEGE OF FRANKING.

Letters and packets to and from the following officers of the government, are by law received and conveyed by post, free of postage.

The president and vice-president of the United States; secretaries of state, treasury, war, and navy; attorney-general; post-master-general, and assistant post-master-general; comptrollers, auditors, registrar, and solicitor of the treasury; treasurer; commissioner of the general land office; commissioners of the navy board; commissary-general; inspectors-general; quarter-master-general; paymaster-general; superintendent of the Patent Office; speaker and clerk of the House of Representatives; president and secretary of the Senate; and any individual who shall have been, or may hereafter be, president of the United States; and each may receive newspapers by post, free of postage.

Each member of the senate, and each member and delegate of the House of Representatives, may send and receive, free of postage, newspapers, letters, and packets, weighing not more than two ounces (in case of excess of weight, excess alone to be paid for), and all documents printed by order of either House, during and sixty days before and after each session of congress.

Post-masters may send and receive, free of postage, letters and packets not exceeding half an ounce in weight; and they may receive one daily newspaper each, or what is equivalent thereto.

Printers of newspapers may send one paper to each and every other printer of newspapers within the United States, free of postage, under such regulations as the post-master-general may provide.

## NEWSPAPERS IN NEW YORK.

Number of newspapers published in this state, according to "Williams's New York Annual Register," in 1831, was 237; 54 in city of New York, and 185 in other parts of the state; 16 daily, and 48 avowedly *anti-masonic*.*

NUMBER OF SHEETS ISSUED FROM THE FIFTY-FOUR PRESSES IN THE CITY OF NEW YORK.

| | |
|---|---|
| Eleven daily papers (average 1,456 each in one day) | 4,944,000 |
| Ten semi-weekly ditto (average 1,880 each in one day) | 1,955,200 |
| Twenty-six weekly ditto | 2,600,000 |
| Six semi-monthly, and one monthly | 36,800 |
| Total number of sheets printed annually | 9,536,000 |
| Estimated number (185 papers) in other parts of the state | 5,000,000 |
| Total | 14,536,000 |

## COPYRIGHT.

Copyright is secured in the United States for fourteen years, by depositing and recording the title of any work, map, chart, &c. at the office of the clerk of the district; and can be renewed by the author, his executors or assigns, at the end of that term, for a further period of fourteen years.—Vide "*Act for the Encouragement of Learning.*" *Judge Story's Statutes of the United States.*

* This has now become a party watch-word, but originated in a just feeling of detestation at a murderous outrage committed by some free-masons a few years ago.

*Number of Bishops in the United States, and their Residences, or Dioceses.*

SIXTEEN PROTESTANT BISHOPS:—viz.

| Dioceses. | Dioceses. |
|---|---|
| Eastern Diocess, or N. England. | Virginia. |
| Connecticut. | South Carolina. |
| New York. | Georgia. |
| New Jersey. | Louisiana. |
| Pennsylvania. | Mississippi. |
| Delaware. | Tennessee. |
| Maryland. | Kentucky. |
| North Carolina. | Ohio. |

Bishops of the Methodist Episcopal Church.

ROMAN CATHOLIC BISHOPS.

| Residence. | | Residence. | |
|---|---|---|---|
| Baltimore - - | Archbishop. | Mobile - - | Bishop. |
| Boston - - | Bishop. | New Orleans - | Do. |
| New York - - | Do. | Bardstown - - | Do. |
| Philadelphia - | Do. | Do. - - | Coadjutor. |
| Do. - - | Coadjutor. | Cincinnati - - | Bishop. |
| Charleston - - | Bishop. | St Louis - - | Do. |

One Archbishop, nine Bishops, and two Coadjutors.

THE END.